Life on the Divide

AF485025

LIFE ON THE DIVIDE

A Two-Wheeled Adventure of Self-Discovery

Mary Ehlers

Life on the Divide, Copyright © 2024 by Mary Ehlers

All rights reserved. No part of this book may be reproduced in any manner whatsoever without written permission except in the case of brief quotations embodied in critical articles and reviews.

First Printing, 2024

For Aaron, Joey and Molly

Great Divide Race
Mountain Bike Route

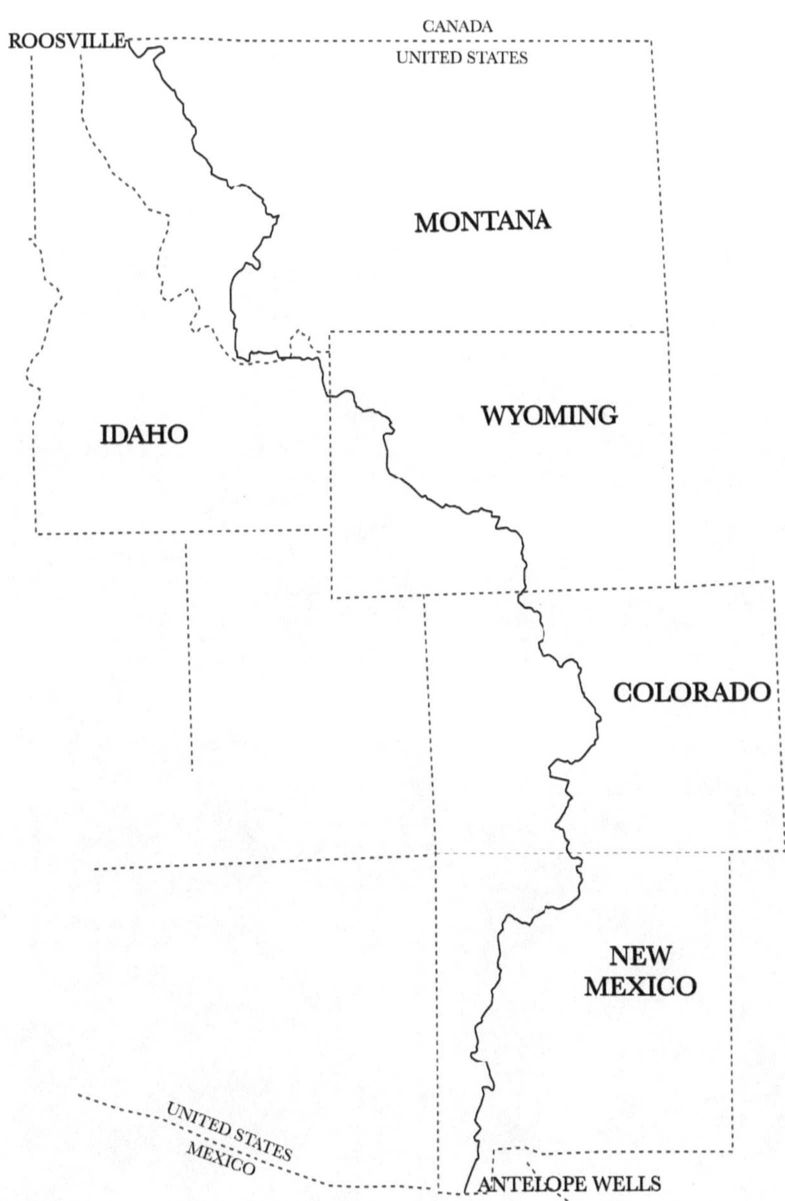

Prologue

Set Goals

At times, my dreams don't always make sense and are hard to explain. When I decided to cycle the Divide, one of the longest off-road cycling routes in the world, it was one of those times. Not knowing what I could accomplish, I set out with one goal: ride my bike for 25 days or 2,500 miles, whichever came first.

The Great Divide Mountain Bike Route, often referred to as the Divide, was developed by the Adventure Cycling Association (ACA) and parallels the Continental Divide from Jasper, Alberta, to Antelope Wells, New Mexico, at the U.S.–Mexico border. The route was established in 1998 as the first cross-country bicycle route of this kind. Although called a mountain bike route, it does not require advanced mountain biking skills as it mostly runs on low traffic roads.

Racing the Divide became popular among a few cyclists in 1999. They set out to race the Great Divide Mountain Bike Route, which at the time ran from Canada to Mexico, and the Great Divide Race was born. Over the next few years, the ACA expanded the route into Canada. In 2008, with fewer than 20 cyclists, a new race was started called the Tour Divide. Starting in Banff, Alberta, outside of

Canada's oldest national park, and finishing at Antelope Wells, the international border crossing, the race covered 2,745 miles.

The Tour Divide is a self-supported bikepacking race. Bikepacking is commonly known as a multi-day bike adventure on which you use your bicycle to carry only the necessities to travel a distance of your choosing. While self-supported bikepacking can be a controversial concept, the idea is to adhere to the principle of completing the ride on your own with no outside support. An individual is limited to using the same resources as others on the route. They must find supplies for themselves, stay on the route and be accountable for their actions.

Riding the Divide can be challenging, as approximately 90% of the route is on unpaved roads or trails from dirt to gravel and riders must cover over 200,000 feet of elevation gain and loss—the equivalent of summiting Everest seven times from sea level. The remoteness and limited food, water and lodging services along the way add to the difficulty.

When the race begins, the Grand Depart, the clock starts and it doesn't stop until you finish. With few rules, racing the Divide is about maintaining the spirit of being a solo self-supported rider, while averaging approximately 100 miles per day to be considered competitive and a "racer." The terrain, weather, trail conditions and distance test your endurance, self-reliance and mental toughness.

With the border closed in 2021 because of COVID-19, I set out to bikepack the original Great Divide Race, from the Canadian border to the Mexican border, covering 2,500 miles across five U.S. states.

This was an experience like no other and yet contained the same elements each day. On the surface, it seems like such a simple concept: ride your bike, find food to eat, find somewhere to sleep, and then repeat for 25 days. The more difficult concepts to convey: the amazing landscapes; the incredible sunrises and sunsets; the starriest of nights; the unbelievable amount of wildlife; the people you meet;

the terrain you ride; and how you handle sleep and food deprivation and the mental challenge of riding when you no longer want to. Ultimately, the Divide is repetitive but maintains its unpredictability, creating a rare opportunity to learn and grow, to see new places, meet new people and put yourself outside of your comfort zone.

My dream of riding the Divide was something I never saw coming, yet it changed my life for the better. The experience taught me how to push myself when my goal seemed beyond my limits or impossible to achieve. It helped me understand what motivates me to keep going and how to channel my emotions to strengthen myself. By the end, I had accomplished something I thought was impossible, leaving me with an overwhelming sense of confidence and pride in myself. I didn't give up when it was hard, and when things seemed unobtainable, I adjusted my goals and kept moving, pushing through the tears.

A Look Back

Love Your Past

ooking back at my childhood, I realize how much the past impacts who I am today. I found a love for the outdoors as a young child. With five brothers and sisters, there was always someone to play with. We would spend time going to the park, having water fights in the backyard or sledding in the winter; we loved spending our days outside. One of the most special memories I have was when I learned to ride a bike. My dad, Papa, would push me up and down the block until I could ride without training wheels.

While those days were happy, they were quickly followed by grief as Papa passed away from cancer. He was only 33 when he was diagnosed. At the time, I had no idea how that would affect my life, as I was just 6 years old. I hardly remember him but from what I can recall, he was a hard-working man who loved to travel, a youth pastor by day and a bartender at night, and always seemed to make time for us kids. Growing up, I always knew I wanted to be just like him.

I remember my mom talking about when he went to Colorado to go backpacking or when he took my brothers to the Boundary Waters Canoe Area. I was jealous that I never got to do those things with him. Those days blur together now, but he spent as much time with us as he could before he passed, and we took advantage of the time we had together. One of my last memories of him is when he came to our kindergarten classroom for Valentine's Day to help make crafts. Every moment counted.

I have this photo in my office, taken before a family road trip, when I got to wake up before the rest of the kids to help pack the van. It was dark outside as we moved the luggage out to the car, but before we finished, the two of us sat on a cooler as my mom snapped a photo of us. I must have felt so special at that moment, thinking of the adventure we were about to embark on to visit Disneyland and the Grand Canyon National Park, not knowing this would be our last family trip with him. I felt sad over the years, like it was unfair that my dad had to die, and I didn't understand why this had to happen to us. I look at that picture now and I'm reminded that our past, good or bad, helps guide our future.

A couple of years later, my mom married Pops. The house was full, with two more kids joining the family. We spent a lot of time at our family cabin, running through the woods, building forts or playing capture the flag. If we weren't running around in the woods, we were swimming in the pool, playing basketball in the driveway or canoeing on the pond. In the winter, we would go sledding or skating, always finding something to do outdoors. The cabin was filled with happy memories, stepping away from our city life, away from the TVs and computers and just enjoying the outdoors and time together.

As I got older, life at home changed. The boys outgrew playing with us but at least I had my twin sister and younger sister. For Christmas one year, our parents got us bikes. I was so excited for a new bike. My birthday fell just a week before Christmas and while I didn't always think I got as many presents as my siblings, this was a really special gift. It was a warm December and we were able to ride them on Christmas Day. There weren't many years we could do that in St. Paul, Minnesota. As we all headed outside to ride bikes with the brisk air on our faces, it was a Christmas I will never forget.

Find Your Passion

When I was in my teens, I was exposed to bicycle touring by a boy named Aaron after we started dating in high school. He was kind, smart and talented. A high school cross-country runner, cyclist and adventurer at only 16. Before he graduated high school he took a group bicycle touring trip to Argentina and then a solo touring trip through northern Minnesota and Michigan. I was so inspired by him that I bought a bicycle and started cycling with him. At such a young age, he already had so much passion and love for the outdoors.

While I was in college, my bicycle was stolen. I was heartbroken. I loved it so much and I thought I would never be able to replace it. So, cycling took a back seat until I could replace my bike, and Aaron and I, now married, started running again. It was much more affordable and took a lot less time and space, which was limited in our one-bedroom apartment. Working full-time jobs while finishing school, we still managed to find time to explore the United States. Aaron would plan trips to the most amazing places, like the slot canyons in Utah or the Grand Canyon. We would hike and run on trails while we visited National Parks, always finding something new to see. I discovered how much I loved to travel, with my best friend by my side. His passion and excitement reminded me of Papa, always wanting to find a new adventure.

In the best way possible, everything changed when we had our children, Joey and Molly, and we loved it. We took family vacations, just like I remembered from when I was a kid, but now I was the mom. Traveling with babies was a lot different, as we had to take more breaks but we adjusted. When Joey was 6 weeks old, we went backpacking in Glacier National Park, carrying little Joey into bear country. It was a fun adventure and a great way to have him snuggled in close while we explored the beauty of the park. A year later, when Molly was 6 weeks old, we hiked with the two in carriers to the highest peak in Colorado. Carrying a toddler and an infant limited how fast we could go, but nothing could completely slow us down.

When we bought our house a few years later, we had space for bikes again, and we were so excited to start riding. I got a road bike and the kids got striders—they couldn't wait to get outside. When the kids were 2 and 3, we decided it was time to try our first family bicycle tour. Not knowing what to expect, we planned a couple of days of riding.

We cycled down the California coast with the kids in tow and more gear than we ever needed. From lost shoes on the highway, camping out under huge trees and even peeing off cliffs on the side of the road, we had the most incredible time. I learned I wasn't good at climbing, but Aaron could do anything. He continued to amaze me with his patience as I was always far behind him, carrying only the sleeping bags and clothes while he had all the heavy gear and two kids in a Burley. He always encouraged me, saying I was doing great. When we finished, we took the Amtrak back to our car, which was a perfect ending to our adventure. Time to sit, reflect and watch the kids' joy as they got to ride in a train for the first time.

Over the next couple of years, we were still running, and I thought I would try to run an ultramarathon because it looked fun when I was watching other people do it. The longest run I had done up to this point was a 10-mile run but I thought, *What's 20 more?* I signed up for a 50K (31 miles) race on the Superior Hiking Trail in Minnesota. I finished with over an hour to spare so I decided to try a 50-mile race on the same trail. I didn't train enough, but once I signed up and was committed, I had to do it. I completed the 50-mile race with minutes to spare on the clock. Exhausted from running and hiking for over 16 hours, I thought, *Maybe this isn't my thing*. So, I tried a winter ultramarathon and signed up for an 80-mile sled pull by foot in Wisconsin. It was mentally hard to be on the snowy trail alone for so long during the cold, dark winter nights and I decided that wasn't my thing either.

Aaron was still running and completed the Lead Challenge in Leadville, Colorado, a race series consisting of six races, best known for the 100-mile bike race followed by a 100-mile foot race the following weekend. After a full summer of both foot and bike racing, he went back to solo bicycle trips.

In 2017, he took on the Trans Am Bike Race, a self-supported bicycle race from the Pacific coast in Astoria, Oregon, to the Atlantic coast in Yorktown, Virginia. I was amazed that anyone could ride their bike 4,200 miles in three to four weeks.

While he was riding, the kids and I packed the car and road-tripped to Virginia. We arrived half a day ahead of him and wandered around the Yorktown Battlefield to keep busy. I felt nervous waiting for him to arrive but thrilled for him to finish something so incredible. As we continued to wait, Joey and Molly ran around as I sat and stared into the sky and tried not to cry; I was so proud of him. When he finally arrived, it felt like a weight was lifted, he was here and safe. While we stood at the finish, under the Yorktown Victory Monument, we met friends he had made during the race and cheered for riders; it was a party with all the excitement of finishing such a huge race. He returned with stories; lifetime friends; and a new love for the long-distance days, beers and camping. Somehow, he convinced me that long-distance biking could be fun.

I began to think the best way to get anywhere was by bike, so when my car needed a minor repair, I chose to leave it at home and start bike commuting. The early, cold mornings in the middle of winter tested me, but riding made my days better. I felt more focused at work and happy that I took some time for myself, realizing that spending a couple of hours commuting helped me to value the time in the evenings at home with our family.

We spent the spring of 2018 planning my first bikepacking trip on the Florida coast, which would be an easy ride since it's so flat. A good friend from the Trans Am joined us, and I spent the week learning what bikepacking was all about. I learned to camp in weird places, bring my bike into hotel rooms and enjoy living in the moment. I finally understood why Aaron loved this so much. The long-mile days meant we got to see more, experience more and not sit around camp for hours, which isn't my thing.

Shortly after our Florida trip, I heard about the North Star Bike Race. I thought trying a short race right from home would be fun. I was familiar with the terrain, which was also a plus. Aaron and I rode together and completed the 630-mile route in just over four days. His patience over the four days of riding helped me to push myself harder than ever before, testing my ability to keep moving when all I wanted to do was sleep.

I started learning more about gravel riding and watched the film "Ride the Divide," which is about the Tour Divide Race. After watching the film, we all knew this was what was next for our family. Before Aaron could finish planning his trip to do the Tour Divide Race, I was already requesting time off from work to pick him up when he was done. I love supporting his dreams, so the kids and I were more than happy to do the long car ride again and have him be gone for another month. We spent the next six months preparing for his race, spending as much time together as possible between training rides.

While preparing for his race, we packed up the car and the kids and headed to Arizona for our first family bikepacking trip. With Joey on his own bike and Molly riding on the back of Aaron's Surly Big Dummy bicycle, what could go wrong? Well, the riding was harder than we anticipated, we ran into many issues with the kids riding on their own, but we learned a lot and had fun camping and enjoying the gorgeous views. The gravel roads were the perfect place to all ride together, to laugh and to make memories.

Then in June 2019, Aaron set out from Banff to ride the Tour Divide, and the kids and I kept busy for two weeks before our road trip. We loaded the car and spent a couple of days driving. Joey got sick on the way down so we thought we would sleep in the next morning, thinking we had plenty of time to drive the last stretch. Instead, we woke up to Aaron calling to let us know he would be at the finish earlier than expected because he had decided to ride all night. We were still an eight-hour drive away so we frantically packed up and hit the road, trying to make as few stops as possible to get to the finish before him.

As we drove down that final stretch of road to the border crossing, the same road the riders were on, the tears started. We hadn't seen him in weeks, and everyone was overwhelmed with joy to be at his finish. It felt a little surreal to be at the Antelope Wells border crossing, in a place we had seen in the film we watched so many times. When we finally saw him, Molly and Joey ran up to him, taking pictures and singing songs. As he biked over to touch the Antelope Wells sign, he took a second to take it all in. With 299.5 miles on the Garmin, he picked up Molly and rode with her on his back, with Joey riding his bike next to him, for the last 0.5 miles to make it a 300-mile day. I smiled with so much joy, taking in what he had just accomplished, so happy that we were able to be there with him.

The moment, the day and everything about it was magical. There were no crowds of people, just us, celebrating. With a beautiful sunset and everything glowing orange, I took his picture, and everything seemed right, his smile saying it all. So proud of him, I laughed and said to him, "There is no way I could ever do this! You look so exhausted and dirty. Why would anyone think this was fun?"

I couldn't stop asking him questions about the race and I didn't know why. It just felt different than after the Trans Am. The stories he told, the people he had met, the areas he had traveled—it was so exciting!

On our drive home we stopped in Salida, Colorado. Just like on our first family tour, we wanted to end the ride with something fun, non-bike related, so our family tradition started: Whenever we are in Salida, we get pizza at Amicas and go to Fun Street Family Arcade for some guaranteed fun.

After we returned from the Tour Divide, I felt inspired and thought I would try the North Star Race again, this time alone. The excitement from the finish of Aaron's ride still had me buzzing. But things didn't go as planned. It rained for the entire first day. It wasn't the rain that bothered me but being on paved roads in the rain. I'm not one to quit things very often—I've done multi-day races before—but the longer I rode through the rain, the harder the day got and the harder it was to hold back the tears.

The fear of road riding and what can come from it started to cause anxiety I didn't know I had. No matter how hard I tried, all I could think about was all the things that could go wrong, and that was the end of my ride. I felt disappointed in myself for quitting when there was nothing wrong. I wasn't sure if bike racing was my thing; I just didn't know what was next.

Aaron was sold on gravel cycling after the Tour Divide, but I still needed convincing, so in January 2020, we decided to try the same Arizona route without the kids. We had a great start and rode over 80 miles on our second day, which felt impressive considering this was a different kind of cycling than in Minnesota or Florida with gravel roads and tons of climbing. Then, on the third day, it rained, and the gravel roads were impossible to ride. That ended our ride, and we enjoyed the rest of our anniversary—yes, this was an anniversary ride—relaxing. I was frustrated we didn't finish but also happy to have learned so much from our short adventure.

Then, just two months later, everything stopped because of the pandemic. No more commuting to work. No more group rides. Hardly any family rides. Aaron's 2020 Tour Divide plans were canceled. The next couple of months went by so fast yet so slowly. I was working at home full time, with both kids doing school at home. Aaron was around a lot more, and at times, we felt trapped in the house. With nowhere to go, it was busy, yet uncomplicated, living. We had no idea if or when we could sign up for races or what the summer would look like.

The kids finished school for the year. Now they were home with nothing to do and nowhere to go while Aaron was off at work and I was still working at home. We did some biking but were cautious, trying to avoid being too close to people. We tried to travel but road-tripping was so different. We decided to get a puppy and he was cute and fun, which helped the rest of the summer pass a little faster. Summer winded down, and we were back to online school. Managing both kids' schooling, my work, a puppy and two bunnies— life was busy.

As winter was approaching and vaccines were coming, we started to look forward to what would be next for biking and our family. From my first bikepacking trip in March 2018 until the second failed attempt at the North Star, I had been bike commuting, going on group rides, and, most importantly, doing family rides. I truly enjoyed having a destination and having my bike be my tool to get me around, which was no longer the case. While I wasn't an excellent rider, I wanted to keep learning, growing and seeing what new adventures my bike could bring.

Aaron was planning on racing the Tour Divide in 2021 after the 2020 race was canceled. We all needed something to look forward to, so this seemed like a great idea. Not knowing what would happen with international travel, the opportunity to ride the U.S. side of the route was still there. That was plan B, with plan A starting in Banff.

He wanted me to go to Banff with him so I could experience the Grand Depart. He told me there was so much energy and excitement in having 100-plus riders gathered in one place to set out to cross the country. You are all starting from zero to see how you compete with those around you. You have different bikes, unique gear and various riding styles. And I think, secretly, he knew seeing the start of the race might be the inspiration I needed to do my own gravel bikepacking race.

After much consideration and knowing how much he wanted me to come along, I agreed. It felt like a huge commitment because I had to find someone to watch the kids, the puppy, the two bunnies, and I needed to get a passport and figure out my travel plans. Plus, I had never traveled alone. There was a lot I needed to do.

As I worked on my plans, Aaron suggested I do a solo bikepacking trip right out of Banff. I could leave with the Grand Depart and ride a week before flying home from Montana. As I looked over the maps and the days off, I thought: *I could do two full weeks off from work—a couple of travel days on both ends and maybe 11 days of riding. With the timing, I could make it home in time for the kids' birthdays. This could work. I am going to try my first solo bikepacking adventure.*

With Papa - 1994 St. Paul, MN

With Joey, Molly and Aaron - 2015 California

Seven Months Before the Divide

Do Something for Yourself

As the days pressed on, I got to thinking: *If I am going to go all the way to the start of the Tour Divide, take two weeks off work, ride for a week and a half, fly home by the kids' birthdays, then work for a week before driving down to the finish to get Aaron, maybe I should do the entire route? Is that even possible for me to do the whole route? I don't know about biking this far, and I've never done a solo trip. What about work? Could I ask for three-and-a-half weeks off? Am I brave enough to say, Hey, can I be gone a month?* I didn't think so.

On top of being gone, we have two kids, a dog, two bunnies, and it was the start of summer break. I knew it would be too much. And what made me think I could do it, anyway? It always seemed like only great cyclists are out racing the Tour Divide, not a mom from St. Paul, Minnesota. I didn't say anything to Aaron because I wanted our focus to be on his race.

But, as the days passed, I couldn't stop thinking about it. I became obsessed with the idea of possibly riding the entire route. It seemed unreal because just two years earlier, I had told myself I would never be able to do this ride. Why did I think I could do it now? I wasn't training or doing anything different. Maybe I needed something to look forward to again after pausing most of our life plans for a year because of the pandemic. Perhaps I just needed my own adventure.

Day after day, I considered riding the Divide. I started looking at the elevation profile, calculating that if I did XX miles, it would take me XX days. I downloaded Aaron's stats from his Tour Divide and compared his miles to days. Once I thought I could do the miles, I pulled all his stats for the elevation. I divided the total elevation by miles to find something like 56 feet per mile. I pulled up my 87-mile-long ride from our Arizona trip and calculated 72 feet per mile. But that was only one day of riding, so could I do more miles, day after day, which the Divide would require? I had never done anything even remotely close to this. I had never camped alone, biked alone in the middle of nowhere, or done anything alone really.

When I finally felt convinced I could do the ride, I had to convince myself that I could miss the kids' birthdays. I love birthdays, specifically my kids' birthdays, because for one day, I get to celebrate Joey, who made me a mom, and Molly, who made me a "girl mom." They changed my life and they love me unconditionally despite all my faults. This was a hard and complicated conversation to have with myself. After spending over a year together during COVID-19, I finally decided that if ever there was a time to give myself a month off, now was it.

I finally told Aaron about my new plan. I said, "What about instead of riding for 11 days, I just do the entire route?" He was totally on board and told me he would make it work if I could get the time off. Then the thoughts started. *Would I feel guilty, like a bad mom, sister or friend? Maybe it's selfish to step away from our home and family. Is it fair to leave my coworkers to cover for me for a few weeks? Or, is it time I do something for myself? And not feel guilty doing something for myself and only myself?* After much consideration, I decided it was my time, and if I'm riding for 11 days, why not try the entire route?

While I still wasn't sure I could complete the entire route, Aaron thought I could. He said, "It might be hard, but it's doable. It would be just over 100 miles a day. You can do that." Plus riding the Divide felt like it should be different than other races because there is no limit for how many days you can be out there pedaling your bike. When I had done the North Star race, I felt pressured to finish within a set amount of time and it was stressful. This time I would be able to ride for as many days as I was able to take off of work. So I decided, I would ride my bike as far as possible and see what I could accomplish.

I sat at my work desk, contemplating how to ask my boss. I didn't know whether to call, email or ask over IM. Should I be formal or casual? I was so nervous that I typed the message repeatedly, trying to figure out what to say. Finally, I decided to ask casually in a mid-morning conversation. I jokingly asked, "Could I ever take three weeks off?" While I thought the conversation might go differently, he said, "Yeah, give me a heads-up, and that should be fine." *Wait, what just happened? Did I get the days off? Wait, do I even want to do this? Or did it all seem like a fun idea until now when I could do it?*

Aaron got home from work, and I said, "You know what I did today? I got the time off work for this summer. The entire three-and-a-half weeks." Immediately, he said, "So you're doing the Tour Divide. I'll skip this year so we can focus on your riding." I was going to ride the Divide.

Always Prepare

The next couple of months were spent preparing for the trip. I began to realize that preparation could mean many things for a bikepacking trip of this magnitude. It took so much time, research and patience that I wondered if I would ever make it to the start. So, I made a list. I needed to prepare to leave home, decide on a bike, pick my gear, make my bags, determine my sleep system, physically train my body, learn the route and mentally prepare for the adventure.

Home

There were so many things to take care of, but the most important was ensuring we had someone to help watch the kids while Aaron was at work. While I thought it would be difficult to find someone to commit to watching the kids months beforehand, my twin sister, Katie, and her family happily agreed to take them anytime we needed help. They were excited that I was doing the race, so they were more than willing to do whatever to help make it happen. Our family pets also needed caregivers and Katie agreed to take the dog, too. Our neighbors helped with the bunnies while the kids and Aaron traveled to pick me up. I was so grateful for everyone's willingness to lend a hand.

The Bike

Before I began figuring out the little details, I needed to figure out what bike I would ride. I owned three bicycles: a gravel bike, a fat-tire bike and a commuter bike, but none was ideal for the entire route. The gravel bike wasn't a good fit because I would need a mountain bike tire. The fat-tire bike wasn't the best because its foot stance width is wider than a mountain bike and could be uncomfortable on a long trip. While my commuter bike would have been an okay pick, it was a heavy bike and the extra weight could make doing the entire route more challenging. So, I wanted something a little better to ride.

The obvious choice was a Salsa Cutthroat, which has a lightweight carbon frame with excellent geometry that makes for a comfortable ride. It's one of the most common bikes seen on the Divide. But finding a Cutthroat or any bike was a challenge during the first year of the pandemic and the one we could buy was going to need a lot of upgrades to make it work. My second choice was to build a Titanium (Ti) Salsa Fargo. A local bike shop, Angry Catfish Bicycle, just happened to have a frame in my size in stock. A titanium frame is a little heavier, but it offers other great benefits, such as being comfortable and durable. It's often considered a "forever" bike and I loved the idea of a forever bike because for an adventure this big, you have to love your bike forever.

We decided on the Ti Salsa Fargo and that I would assemble the bike myself. Over the next couple of months, we ordered all the parts, from picking the handlebar and cranks to the color accents on the bike. It was stressful at times and finding the parts in stock took a while but it was well worth the wait. Putting together my bike was a great experience because now I had an idea of how things worked if I ever needed to do any maintenance during the ride. I was nervous about the fit and comfort because I was building the bike, but Aaron helped me get the bike's fit dialed in from the saddle height to the stem length so everything felt just right. I was riding my new bike by early spring.

Bags

I started looking at bags—there were so many options. I wanted to see how others carried their gear and what types of bags people liked, as I knew I wanted to make my own. I studied apparel design in school and have pretty good sewing skills. I always said that if I ever took an adventure this big, I wanted to make as many of my own bags as possible, but I still had to be able to get all the gear to fit into those bags.

I spent time drafting patterns, reviewing previous bags I had made, and figuring out what worked and what needed to change. I researched the best materials to use based on weight and waterproofness. I started sewing my bags, and slowly, they came together just as I had imagined.

While researching, I found a bag design I loved by Oveja Negra bikepacking. I tried everything I could to recreate the bag but couldn't figure it out. I reached out to the company and explained how I always imagined making my bags and that I would love to try to make something like theirs, and they offered to sell me the piece I needed. I am so grateful that they were willing to support my dream and help my bag come together.

I had my frame bag, two fork bags, two feed bags and a seat bag all on the bike, and I was ready to test things out to see how they would work. I took the bike for a long ride and quickly realized the seat bag needed work. The distance between the bag and the back tire was too close, and when I hit a bump, I could feel them touch. I made some adjustments to see if I could make it work, but after hours of effort, I ultimately decided the seat bag wouldn't work.

The problem I was having was in my head: It didn't feel like bikepacking if I didn't use a seat bag and had to use a rack instead. I felt so defeated. I didn't want to give up on what I had made, but I also couldn't get hung up on something that wouldn't work. I just didn't have enough room between my tire and my seat for a bag and you *can* bikepack with a rack. So, I moved over to using a rack, came up with a couple more bag ideas and got to sewing.

I had all the bags on the bike and was back to testing. The bike rode great on gravel roads and felt good climbing; it was time to test if the bags would hold up in the rain. So, whenever it rained, Molly would send me out on a ride to test the waterproofness of the bags. I would come home and check for any wet spots, and if I found one, I would repair the bag with more seam seal tape before testing again. The bike bags were all set.

Sleep System

Next, I wanted to sew a sleeping system, which would be my sleeping bag, booties and some type of hat. Before I started sewing, I researched temperature ratings, fabric options and goose down. I ordered the fabric and hydro goose down and got to work. I started by making a down quilt because a full sleeping bag weighs more and takes up more space on the bike. If a quilt worked, I could save a lot of weight and room, which was limited.

Once the quilt was ready, it was time to test. Molly and I slept on the deck in the late winter when the night's lows were similar to what I expected on the ride. After our night out, I realized that the quilt wasn't going to be warm enough, so I ordered more materials and made a mummy-style sleeping bag. The bag was a bit more complicated, but I was able to make the sleeping bag the perfect length and distribute the down where I wanted, adding more to the foot box and less in the hip area to make it the ideal temperature.

By the time I finished the bag, the weather was getting warmer but we still camped out a second night. It was early spring, so I wasn't sure it got cold enough to test the rating, but everything seemed to work much better than on the first night. I made a pair of down booties and a down hood for a little extra warmth. Down booties are popular but I hadn't seen a lot of down hoods, and it worked perfectly. A hat or buff would have also worked, but they usually fall off when I'm sleeping, and I made the hood like a pullover hoodie, so it wasn't going anywhere. The process of making the sleeping bags was slow but fun and very rewarding.

Gear

I went back and forth on whether to take a bivy shelter (a low-rise tent for a single person) or a single-person tent. The bivy is a much lighter weight option and takes up less space on the bike. It also takes a lot less time to set up, so I decided on that. As much as I wanted to make a bivy, I didn't want to be cold and wet in the middle of nowhere and mad because I didn't seam seal it correctly, so I opted to use an Outdoor Research bivy.

For fun, I made a couple of clothing items, some riding tights, a down jacket and a fleece sweater. I used Pearl Izumi bib shorts as I didn't want to mess with padded shorts. I researched what to use for a rain jacket and decided on a heavier jacket for the extra warmth instead of a lightweight rain jacket.

I researched the best options for navigation, Garmin vs. Wahoo, and decided to use a Wahoo for its simplicity and larger screen. I worked through how I would charge my electronics. I planned to use a dynamo hub, which was built into my front wheel. When the wheel turns, the electronic generator in the hub can charge small electronic devices, such as my headlight or a Wahoo. I also carried a couple of portable chargers for backup power.

I would carry a stove so I could make hot water for coffee and simple foods like oatmeal and ramen. I created a repair kit, found a first aid kit and gathered all my bike tools.

After I had mostly everything I needed, I started to figure out how to fit it all on the bike. This was challenging at times, trying to make the most of the space, like playing a game of Tetris. Once I decided how I liked it, I made a list of what was in each bag so I could remember where everything went when I had to unload it.

Physical Preparation

Aaron offered two pieces of great advice. 1. Ride your bike every day. Even if it's a short ride, it will be good to be in the rhythm of riding every day. 2. Ride it fully loaded. Training with it loaded meant I could feel how heavy the bike was and I was able to make sure all the gear fit just right in the bags, and that is exactly what I did.

My training rides mainly consisted of short, 10- to 30-mile rides around town or with the family. I also tried to hop on my indoor trainer for 30 to 60 minutes most days. I worked in a couple of 50- and 100-mile rides, but finding time for an entire day's ride was hard because once it got nice out, I wanted to spend as much time as possible with the kids before I left. I tried to find hills around the city to do repeats on to see how climbing with the heavier bike would feel, knowing that this would still be easy compared to the Divide. I couldn't ride as much as I would have liked, but I did as much as I could.

In addition to riding, I got up at 5:30 a.m. and did an app workout. This was good training to prepare my body to wake up early. I was able to use those six months to focus on losing some of the weight I had put on during that first year of COVID-19. The less weight I had to carry over every mountain pass, the better. While St. Paul isn't the best training ground for the Divide, I did my best to balance family and training needs.

Route Research

Even though we were following the Great Divide Mountain Bike Route, there is more to it than following the map. There can be detours or small route changes every year. I wasn't sure my pace would be the 100 miles per day I needed to be considered a racer, but I still wanted to follow the race route. Using a navigation device like a WahooRoam, I would be able to follow the route from my bike computer. I also carried a personal satellite GPS device, SPOT, which allowed me to share my location through the Trackleaders website. The route would be uploaded and my SPOT device would show my location as a dot on the screen, like a "breadcrumb," for my family and friends to follow along while I was riding.

I spent a lot of time studying the maps to get a good understanding of the distance between towns and the services available. This was important because this route is remote, and you may only see one town every 100 or more miles. Since I planned to ride around 100 miles a day, this could leave me in random places camping before or after towns. I planned to get my miles in every day; even if I was in a town at dinner time, I planned to keep riding until the end of the day. My goal was to ride the route in 25 days. I needed to stay on this pace as much as possible so I wanted to carry enough food and water to get me to the next town, plus a little extra for emergencies. I wanted to be as lightweight as possible but able to survive if I encountered poor weather, mechanical issues, injury or an unrideable section where I had to push my bike. There were many situational pieces to consider, so it was essential to understand the route.

I spent hours reviewing, mainly what Aaron had done, because I was trying to do something similar. I looked at his distance and elevation gain to better understand what I was facing. I downloaded the OneofSevenProject town list sheets, which provided distances to towns and services for the Tour Divide. I combined the information from the lists and the ACA maps and created my cue sheets with all the information I deemed necessary. I kept a downloaded version on my phone for quick access and used the ACA app as a backup.

Then it was decided, since no one knew when the border would open, that the route would start in the United States at the border in Montana. I was really sad for a while, disappointed that I wouldn't be able to complete the entire route since I would miss the Canadian section. But the reality was, I didn't get to make the decision and I needed to keep moving forward with planning. So I revamped everything. Aaron and I discussed good places to stay and hotel options, but starting at noon and 250 miles south of where he had, meant it would be a very different race.

Mental Preparation

I wasn't scared to fail, but I needed to be prepared to ride my bike alone, in the middle of nowhere, camping alone, figuring everything out for myself for 25 days, all while remaining safe. The only way I knew how to do that was to believe I could do it, even when I wasn't sure if I could. I told myself every day for six months that I could. I hoped that this attitude would be enough to push me through the hard moments that I knew were coming. Some days, I believed in myself, while other days, I wasn't sure. The most important thing was that every day, I had the support of my family. Aaron knew the route and had confidence in my abilities even when I wasn't sure of myself.

I chose not to share my plans with many people beforehand, not because I was scared of letting people down if I didn't finish, but because I didn't want anyone to put any doubt in my head, put me down or make me feel bad for taking time for myself. The more I thought about what I was about to do, the more I felt like people would judge me. The thought of anyone having any opinion about me riding made me scared to tell anyone.

Everything was coming together. Tickets were purchased, and every detail I could think of, from the arrangements for the kids and pets to who would get the mail, was taken care of. The bike was perfect, and the bags and gear fit exactly how I wanted. I was riding my bike, training my body and mentally preparing to ride 2,500 miles.

Two Days
Before the Divide

It's Okay to be Sad

My emotions were all over the place leading up to the moment when I finally boarded the plane to Montana. I was anxious about flying and my bike and gear all making it. I had a pit in my stomach, wondering if I had forgotten anything. I was excited that it was almost here, but I wasn't ready to say goodbye to my kids. I had never left them for four weeks; they were not used to Mom leaving. They were finally old enough to know how long a month felt.

My parents drove Aaron and me to the airport, and the kids rode with Katie. I nervously stared out the window at everything so familiar, feeling like I had when I left home for the first time to go to college. I asked myself what I was doing.

When we arrived at the airport, it started pouring. The rain came out of nowhere, but I needed a picture with my parents so my mom snapped a photo of me and Pops with huge smiles. My mom sent me the photo, and it quickly reminded me of the moment I had as a child with Papa sitting on that cooler, ready for a big trip. Now years later, I was having my own adventure, and to have my parents sending me off meant so much.

We moved the bikes inside so the cardboard wouldn't get damaged. Molly had decorated the box, and it was so cute I didn't want her work to get ruined. I also needed to protect the boxes and keep them as dry as possible before the flight, so I quickly hugged my parents goodbye, and with every moment, I started to feel a little more nervous. I couldn't help but worry about something happening. I was almost hugging the box because I needed the bike to make it in one piece with nothing broken. We stood in line, waiting to check the bikes in, and then the TSA agent opened the box for inspection. Everything was good—what a relief—so we headed to the top floor of the parking ramp to meet Katie and the kids.

The parking ramp was quiet, with no cars on the top floor. I knew it would be emotional for everyone, so having a moment at the airport without crowds was a better way to say goodbye. I hugged my nephews, Fitz and Owen, and they returned to running around the parking ramp. Joey and I had a little chat and a nice side hug—all I could get from him at this age—and then he was off. Katie ran over to hug me while chasing the kids. Then Aaron, Molly and I sat on a curb and snuggled, and the tears started flowing. We were all so excited about what I was about to do, but also sad that we would be apart from each other for so long. We tried to make light of the moment and had a couple of laughs, but when it was finally time to go, I walked away from my baby with tears falling down her face. She was happy and sad simultaneously, and I just had to keep going. I turned away and put on my face mask before heading to the gate.

After the short flight to Montana, I was overjoyed when we disembarked onto the runway. It was like something you see in the movies; I couldn't believe I got to do that in real life. I was smiling from ear to ear, telling Aaron how cool it was—like no one had ever done it before. Waiting inside the airport, I was uneasy until my bike was finally wheeled out with the oversized luggage.

We arrived after midnight and had a hotel near the airport. We planned an early start the following day as we would bike the 70 miles to our hotel just outside of Roosville, Montana, near the start of the race. Leaving the airport, we saw another rider. He told us his plane had been delayed; he got in three hours later than he had planned and needed to figure out where he would stay. We offered to let him sleep in our hotel room since we had two double beds. *A little good karma,* I thought. The excitement of seeing another rider was nice, but I still felt like I had so much to do, and all I wanted to do was get some rest. It was starting to feel real, but the best news was that one of the most nerve-wracking pieces was over: We had made it to Montana with my bike.

We woke up the following day to rain. Aaron offered to ride to REI for me and pick up the bear spray I had ordered so I could relax and not get soaked. As the rain continued, we checked the weather, and Aaron graciously arranged a ride to the hotel so I didn't have to bike 70 miles in the rain and I was able to keep all my things dry for at least one more day. Don't get me wrong, I knew I would need to ride in the rain at some point, but I wasn't ready to be wet yet.

It was a long car ride through northern Montana, so I was happy with our choice. When we finally arrived, we could relax. After an afternoon nap, I woke up frantic, feeling like I had so much to do. Even though all my gear was right in front of me, and I knew how I wanted to pack the bike, I felt overwhelmed. I just stared at it, hoping it would pack itself, but I had to start loading the bike. After one more check to make sure nothing had fallen under the bed, I took the bike out for a quick spin through the resort to ensure everything was alright. I wanted the morning to be leisurely and, ideally, to have no more adjustments to make. We sat down for dinner and met another rider from Minnesota; it was exciting to know that other people were from my home state. We spent the rest of the evening in the hot tub before calling it a night. I thought it might be hard to sleep, but I was exhausted from all the travel and being nervous and excited. I was ready to ride the Divide.

THE GREAT DIVIDE

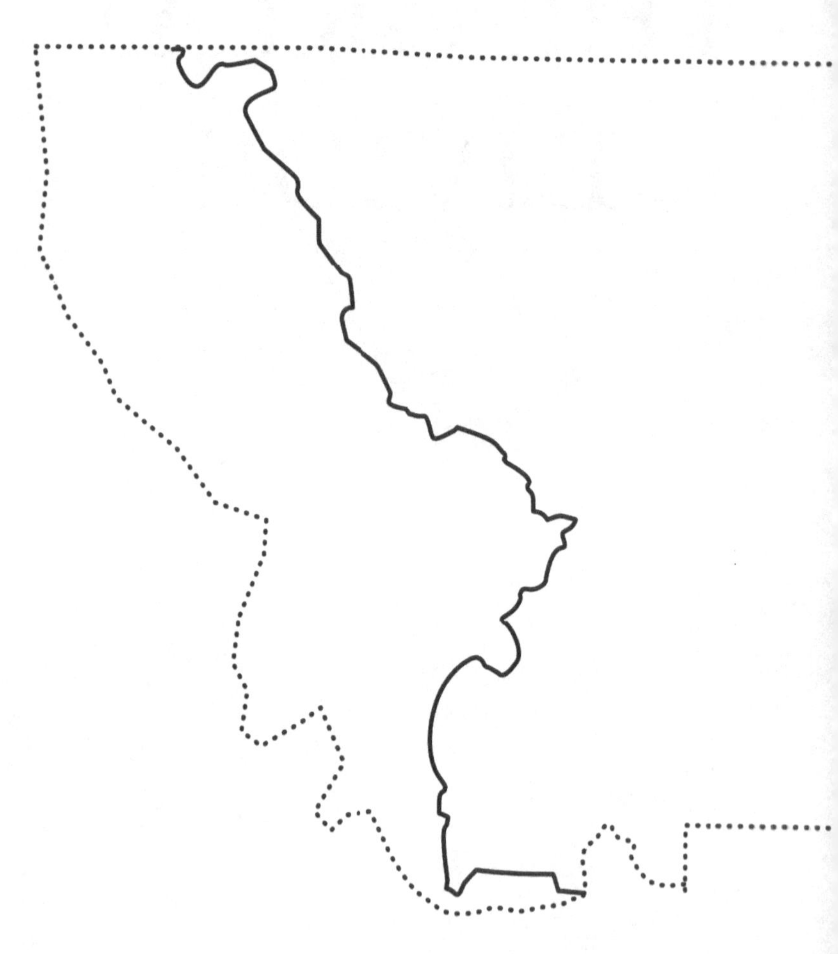

Montana

Be Patient

Day 1 The Grand Depart was at noon. After a 10-mile ride, Aaron and I arrived at about 11 a.m., snapped photos at the border crossing and chatted with riders before heading to the start area. There were so many people. It seemed unbelievable to be among all these cyclists and to think we were all going to the same place—Mexico! I became anxious and self-conscious as I looked at their bikes, gear and clothing choices. *Am I ready? Can I do this? These people look like legit bikers,* I thought. *What am I doing here? Am I in over my head?* I could do nothing now but get out of my head and have fun.

I gave the kids one more FaceTime call, hugged Aaron and approached the crowd. Anxiously looking around, I spotted my fellow Minnesotan from dinner. I walked over to him and, seeing his bike, realized he was the rider I had heard about before coming out here. I remembered seeing him on a training ride with his bike fully set up.

As we stood there, a couple of minutes before noon, I frantically tried to get my Wahoo navigation device going while trying to remain calm. I thought, W*hy did I wait so long to turn it on?* I started to feel nervous, but I didn't need to; I only needed to ride my bike. I kept thinking of all the things I had never done, and the two things that kept popping into my head were that I had never camped alone nor ridden back to back to back long days on gravel roads. I could hardly hear whoever was talking up front, distracted by my thoughts and everything going on, and then, just like that, we started riding.

I stayed toward the back of the group, and those first miles to Eureka, Montana, were so fun and fast. Aaron rode with me for a couple of minutes before he turned right, and I went left. I waved goodbye, holding back tears, but this was it. It was my time. There was so much excitement, and everyone was talking and smiling. I got to Eureka quickly and picked up lunch and dinner at Subway. Heading out of Eureka, the goal for the day was to make it as far as possible, maybe to Whitefish, Montana. Starting at noon made it feel like I was losing four hours of good pedaling time, aka daylight, so I just had to do my best.

There were many days ahead of me, and although I didn't want to "lose" too many miles on day one, I also wasn't sure exactly what I was getting myself into. I needed to be patient and ride my pace. I started up the first climb, which was very gradual. I was on paved roads for a while, which was frustrating because I was ready for gravel, so it felt weird to be riding this perfectly paved road for so long. Then, it turned into gravel and I thought, *I'm riding the Divide.*

After only a couple of hours I was already tired, which made me laugh since it was the first day of biking. I pulled over for a snack and a nap. I couldn't believe I was napping on day one, but with many days to go, I needed to take care of myself. As I neared the top of the climb, I started biking with some guys Aaron had met at the start. They were kind and planned to tour and were going to ride shorter mile days than I was, so they slowed down and rode with me for a while, since they were in no rush. It was nice to have some people to chat with for a while, after all that was the point of starting with the Grand Depart. After descending, they headed to a camping spot, and I pushed on.

I was onto the second climb, which was again very gradual, and I felt so slow because I was already tired. This was only the second or third time I had biked this far with any amount of climbing, and my body and mind were already drained. I looked at the map for what felt like the 50th time and decided I needed to make it to the campground near the top. I was exhausted. All I wanted to do was sleep and I thought, *I need to figure out how I will do this all again tomorrow*. I wanted to reach the campground no matter what, so I started walking and pushing my bike. I pushed for almost 3 miles. It felt wrong to be pushing my bike on the first day, but walking is also forward progress, so I focused on that.

It was starting to get dark and I could feel the temperature drop as I approached the campground. With snow on the ground, I knew it would be a cold night and I was hoping my sleeping bag and liner would be warm enough. There were a lot of other riders at the campground; it was nice to find other people, especially in bear country. I got there late, so I unpacked my food into the bear box and chatted with a couple of folks for a brief moment. I set up my bivy away from where everyone else was camping to ensure that if they hadn't gotten their food off their bikes, I wasn't too close to them. I got in bed, trying not to waste any time. I was a little bummed that I hadn't accomplished the distance I was hoping for, but I was also ready to call it a day. As I lay there, I started thinking, *How can I do this again and again?* I had traveled just over 70 miles and was exhausted as I fell asleep in mid-thought.

June 11: Roosville, MT, to Red Meadow Campground, MT

Route Mileage: 0 – 72.2

Distance: 72.2 miles

Elevation Gain: 5,814 feet

Kindness Still Exists

Day 2 I tossed and turned all night, listening to the rain through my bivy. It was still drizzling as my alarm went off, and my first thought was to see if the rain would stop. It was nice and warm inside my bivy and waiting for the rain meant I could stay in there a little longer. But I had to get moving, rain or no rain. I packed up my sleeping bag and bivy as quickly as possible to avoid getting things wet that should be dry, but with the bivy soaked, I just had to do my best to keep my sleeping bag dry. I hurried to the pit toilet and parked my bike under the cover while getting food from the bear box. It was nice to have a moment to rearrange my things without getting wet.

As I was preparing to leave the campground, some of the riders were just starting to get up. I headed down the trail, which was covered in a wet snow that forced me to walk. The snow was mushy from the rain, so I walked fast to stay warm.

It kept raining for hours and trying to stay warm became a challenge. I was on and off the bike, trying not to let my hands or feet get too cold. Already feeling frustrated about my miles and now the rain, I needed to find a way to get some positivity into my day because I wasn't happy.

As I started down a descent into Whitefish, my feet were soaked and freezing. I had tried to keep my feet dry by putting plastic bags over my socks but that didn't work. I changed my socks under a tree and put new bags on, and that seemed to help a little, but then my hands got cold because I stopped for too long. I tucked them inside my rain jacket and just hoped it would stop raining.

As I kept moving slowly down the descent, the hard rain turned into a drizzle just a couple of miles before I got to town. I checked the weather and saw that the rain would end very soon, so I took some time in Whitefish to get breakfast, try to warm up and charge my phone and Wahoo. Sitting at the breakfast bar, I was in tears, cold, frustrated and trying to understand how I could keep going if I had more days like this. I couldn't believe I was already so upset; I was only on the second day and had 23 more days ahead of me. It was hard to imagine that I had to keep going again and again. After a yummy and very sugary breakfast, the rain stopped and my mood shifted a little. With some food and a little sunshine, I was feeling hopeful.

As I made my way out of town, the weather was improving, and the sun was trying to shine through the clouds. The riding was easy on some pavement, yet I felt slow, tired and not very excited about biking. I couldn't figure out what was going on with me and why I wasn't having fun. I really needed to figure this out.

As I got into Columbia Falls, Montana, I was looking for a place to pick up some snacks when I met a group of riders. I thought that maybe I could ride with them and that would lift my spirits. Unfortunately, I was still trying to find somewhere to get some food when they left town. Thinking maybe I could catch up with them, I told them I'd see them down the road and continued alone. When I checked my map, I noticed I had biked past all the grocery stores in town. I found a gas station and was headed there instead, only to realize it was 1 mile past the route when I arrived. I was frustrated, but there was nothing I could do about it now.

The sun finally came out and the clouds were dissipating. I was warming up and looking forward to a late lunch at the Echo Lake Café, which closed at 2:30 p.m. I wanted to get something to eat and use the bathroom since I had gotten my period that morning.

Continuing down the road to Echo Lake Café, I saw some people out cheering. They're known as "Dotwatchers" because they watch the Trackleaders web page to see when riders would come by. The first set of people I saw had a big sign in their yard that said something like "2,386 miles to Antelope Wells." I knew I was only on day two and about 100 miles in, but I teared up when I saw it. Something about seeing that sign made it feel real again. I had been to the finish to pick up Aaron, and I could already picture myself riding up to the big Antelope Wells sign. It gave me the feeling that I would make it. I thought, *Yes, things can happen, but assuming nothing happens, you're gonna do it*. I was more confident than ever about this ride. It was so exciting and nerve-wracking because just hours ago, I had been cold, tired, hungry and unsure.

An hour later, I saw a man and two young girls outside with cowbells. They asked, "Are you Mary from Minnesota?" I replied yes and waved to them, and they started cheering. I teared up again as I rode away, thinking how cool it was to have these young girls, about the same age as my daughter, see a woman out here riding. I regretted not stopping and talking to them.

I pulled up to the Echo Lake Café with 10 minutes to spare. I quickly ordered food, and in the bit of sunshine I could find, I laid out my sleeping pad, sleeping bag and bivy to dry. As I ate my lunch, I felt so disappointed in myself and sad that I hadn't stopped when people were out cheering. It was so kind and thoughtful of them but I had just kept biking. I had no reason to hurry away except that I had been so focused on making it to the cafe that I wasn't thinking about anything else.

I finished lunch and started back down the road. I was moving slowly. One by one, a group or a person would come by, and

I would say a quick hello and keep moving. As I approached the top of a climb, a couple of riders were right behind me. Embarrassed by how slowly I descend, I let them pass so I could take my time.

As I started into the next section, it was getting dark in the heavy tree-covered woods, but I started one more climb with the little daylight I had left. I was tired and moving slowly but I was making my way up the climb when I saw a group of riders who said I could camp with them. It was just before 8:30 p.m. and I thought I needed to keep going. I knew I would be able to ride until at least 9 or 10 most nights and I needed those extra miles. I kept slowly biking and walking until I made it about 5 more miles up the climb and found another group of riders who said I could camp with them. It was dark now, the sun had set and it was after 9:30 p.m. I had 100 miles in for the day, and it seemed like a great spot.

I set down my bike and went over to the picnic table. I sat and chatted with the riders—Gyorgy, Erik, Chris, Bobby and Joe— while they all cooked dinner. I was confused about why they were eating right before bed, but I hung out briefly anyway before setting up camp. I grabbed my food from my bike, as we all agreed to put it together on the picnic table, away from where we were sleeping. It was time for bed, so I climbed into my bivy, set my alarms and checked over the maps one more time before falling sound asleep.

June 12: Red Meadow Campground, MT, to N. Swan Lake informal campground, MT

Route Mileage: 72.2 – 175.62

Distance: 103.41 miles

Elevation Gain: 5,412 feet

Don't Let Fear Get the Best of You

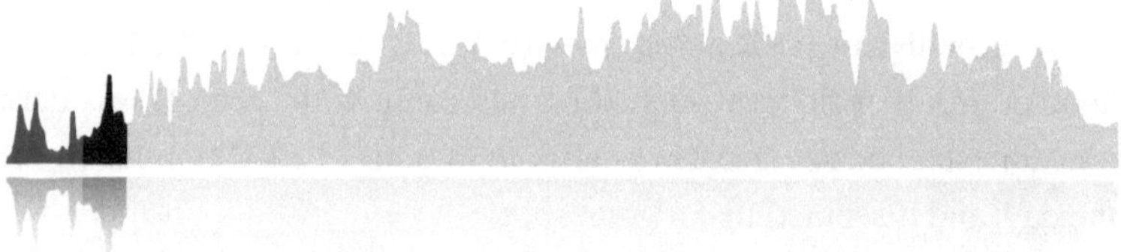

Day 3 When my alarm went off, I realized no one else was awake so I quickly got out of my bivy. I packed my gear and I was ready to head back to the trail when I started to hear everyone else moving. I managed to leave camp before anyone was out of their tents and bivvies, but I knew they would catch up with me later that day.

I was enjoying the quiet morning with the sun shining through the leaves, the birds chirping and everything glowing yellow in the woods when I saw a large white dog cross the trail. I paused for a moment and thought, *Wait, that makes no sense, a dog out here in the middle of the woods.* I stopped and stood next to my bike, confused about what I had just seen. I thought, *What had just walked across the trail?* Then I realized it wasn't a dog at all. I wasn't positive but maybe it was a mountain lion or a wolf. I waited a couple of minutes so it would have time to get into the woods. Feeling a little nervous, I went down the trail on high alert as I didn't want to see that animal again. I was prepared to see bears, but I had never considered seeing any other large animals. I thought, *Whatever that was, I hope this is the only one I see.*

The morning riding was great and I was feeling a lot better than I had the day before. After a couple of hours riding, the group I had camped with the night before caught up to me. They said they had heard that same animal in the woods when they went by. It was nice to know I wasn't losing it or seeing random dogs walking across the trail in the middle of the woods.

I was excited to get real food for lunch, as I had looked up the hours for Holland Lake Lodge the night before to make sure it would be open. The lodge was a little over a mile off the route; I didn't want to waste my time going there if it was going to be closed.

I rode with the group for a while and it was nice to have some people to talk with. They were also planning to stop at Holland Lake Lodge for lunch, which forced me to ride a little faster than I normally did so I could eat with them. When we arrived at the lodge, we found out the kitchen was closed for "deep cleaning."

We asked if they could open the gift shop so we could at least get some snacks before heading back to the route. I was very frustrated because I really wanted some lunch before an afternoon of climbing. The staff offered us ham-and-cheese or peanut butter-and-jelly sandwiches and chips so I at least got something for lunch and I thought, *Good enough.*

I took my food over to a bench next to the lake to relax and eat while I enjoyed a beautiful backdrop—a picture-perfect blue sky over the snow-capped mountains by a crystal-clear lake. I finished my lunch and went to pay the bill. Surprisingly, they charged me as if I had eaten a full meal from their menu, which seemed odd since it was a ham-and-cheese sandwich, but that made for a good laugh. Just as I was packing up the bike with some candy from the gift shop, a second group of riders showed up. Then, as we were leaving, a third group rolled in. The lodge picked the wrong day to "deep clean" the kitchen.

After lunch, the guys took off ahead of me, and I climbed up Richmond Peak alone. I was still trying to get used to all this climbing because it was so much longer and harder than I anticipated. When I neared the top, the trail turned from a gravel road onto some single track. I took a minute to look out over the valley at the sun high in the sky over the beautiful forest below me, and I couldn't believe I was here doing this. I felt so lucky.

As I turned down the single track, there started to be small patches of snow. The wet snow, slowly melting from the hot sun, covered more and more of the trail until it was time for some hike-a-biking. It was too mushy for me to ride so I kept pushing my bike. The trail would clear of snow and I would think I could ride, and then there would be another long stretch of snow-packed trail and I would have to walk. I turned and looked out over the valley again, but this time I saw an afternoon storm out in the distance.

As I approached the top, the trail finally cleared of snow. I still had to walk my bike through a little more of the single track because I was nervous about the drop-off on my left side. I was not prepared for single track, especially on top of a peak. I continued to push my bike, thinking: *I do not have technical bike skills, and this is terrifying, and the storm is getting closer. You have to move faster Mary.* I kept pushing, working through the single track as quickly as possible when the rain started. I was finally on the downhill, which opened up to a smooth gravel road. I was so relieved to be on a surface I felt comfortable on again, even in the rain. I quickly descended on the road until the route moved me back to some more single track.

I hopped off the bike and started pushing it because the trail was covered with downed branches and trees, but in this wide-open area the trail had huge dips that were tough to get through. I had to lift my bike, which was heavy and awkward for me to do. I kept tripping on the bike and falling over, hitting my shins on the pedals. I was a mess.

It started lightning but at least now it was only a light rain. Then, as I was standing, just trying to figure out what I should be doing, I looked into the woods and saw five trees fall. I was so scared. I didn't know if I should be near my bike, in the woods, or what. I thought I knew what to do in a storm, but the reality of being in one scared me, more than I thought it would.

I tried calling Aaron and Katie, but no one answered. I just wanted to hear someone's voice. Finally, my brother-in-law Brian answered and helped calm me down. Just as I started back down the trail, two riders came up behind me, and I stuck with them until the storm passed. The storm only lasted 30 minutes, but it felt like a lot longer as I was more scared than I thought I would be. It wasn't as life-threatening as it seemed, and it was a good reminder to stay calm when things feel out of my control.

As I popped out of the woods, I looked over and saw some pavilions off to the right. I considered staying there the night, but I decided to keep going to the next town, Ovando, Montana, and camp out there. I was thinking the group of guys I had camped with the night before had pressed on and I would see them in Ovando in the morning.

I kept riding down the road and as the sun set, I got tired and it got dark quickly. Riding at night was tricker than I had thought it would be. In my first few days, I didn't ride too late into the night, and it felt odd that I was only three days in and I was already this tired. I was already using all my tricks to stay awake. I had two lights running, I was singing songs and I was eating peach rings. I kept telling myself I could still make it to Ovando if I just kept pedaling.

Then, as I looked into the woods, I saw a mountain lion staring at me. This time I knew it was a mountain lion. The eyes of that cat, just peering down at me, followed my movement down the road. My heart pounded, and my energy level shot up. I pushed my bike on my left with my bear spray close by in my right hand, and once I felt comfortable, I hopped back on and rode as quickly as I could. I kept moving down the road and saw a couple more eyes looking at me. I thought, *Keep moving, and hopefully, they won't come chase me*. Every couple of minutes, I would look over my shoulder to make sure nothing was following me. This helped keep me alert for the last miles into Ovando.

I finally made it to Ovando, exhausted, and looked for the camping area. I checked my map and tried to understand where to stay, but I was struggling to find the campground area in the dark. I looked around and picked a spot next to a tree outside a little building in the middle of town. I was so tired, I didn't even care if that wasn't where I should camp. I just wanted to be done for the day, so I laid out my bivy, crawled in and started looking over my cue sheet for the next day. I set my alarms, but it was already 1 a.m. so I thought I'd sleep in until 6 a.m., and I quickly reset the alarms before falling asleep.

June 13: Swan Lake informal campground, MT, to informal camping in Ovando, MT
Route Mileage: 175.62 – 277.45
Distance: 101.83 miles
Elevation Gain: 10,732 feet

Tough Times can Bring You Together

Day 4 When I woke up, I realized I had forgotten to check the hours for the little shop in town. Since it didn't open until 7 a.m., I decided to sleep a little longer. After snoozing my alarm several more times, I finally decided to get moving and headed to the shop for food, water and a bathroom. I saw some other riders waking up, but none were the guys from yesterday. I assumed maybe they had camped after Ovando and I might not see them again. I had only met them two days ago, and it would have been nice to make some friends. But I reminded myself I was here to ride alone.

I headed over to the shop to grab pastries and snacks for the day and finally left town around 8 a.m. I was grateful the shop had a public restroom; I was already realizing how nice a restroom was. It was a late start to my day, which made me a little impatient, but then I remembered I had biked until 12:30 a.m. and a little extra sleep was good for my body.

Leaving town, the riding was uneventful with good weather and no wildlife sightings, just what I needed. I had done back-to-back 100-mile days, and I was really proud of myself. I thought maybe I could do one more 100-mile day. I looked over the maps and saw a larger town with a hotel. Maybe I could make it there. The idea of sleeping in a hotel and taking a little break from the routine of setting up and taking down camp had me really excited.

The road was smooth, the sun was shining, and I was pedaling along, listening to a book, and enjoying my peaceful morning. As the sun's heat became more intense, I started to feel really warm and the road didn't have any trees close enough for shade. Feeling hot, I found a small patch of shade under a tree, in the ditch, and decided I needed to take a break because I was not feeling good. I had been riding a little faster than normal all morning, worrying about the late start to my day and excited about possibly getting to a hotel.

I was lying down in the ditch, and a rider passed and checked in to make sure I was doing okay. Everyone was so kind to each other out here. I was starting to feel better, and then two touring cyclists came by and asked how I was doing. I told them I was just taking a break and they said I should ride with them. I explained how slow I was going, and they said it didn't matter because they weren't in a hurry. I was happy to have some company, so I got up and moving, and we biked together.

I asked them about their trip and they told me how one of them had wanted to do more touring but didn't have a riding friend, so he asked the other guy, who wasn't even a cyclist, to join him and he agreed. I asked the non-cyclist if he loved it yet, and he said "Yes!" It reminded me of when Aaron took Molly and my brother touring on a section of the ACA Southern Tier Route; it was my brother's first bicycle tour trip. Aaron loves taking people on cycling adventures and introducing them to this world we love. He always tells them that he'll ride at their pace and carry the gear because he doesn't want them to hate it—he'll do whatever it takes to make them love it. These two riders made me so happy and lifted my spirits. I love when people try cycling and love it.

We turned the corner and before we started to head up the next climb, we stopped at a small creek. I decided to filter some water and take a nap. They were going to soak in the creek and said I should, too, since it was so hot out, but I hate being in wet clothes, so I decided a nap in the shade would be better.

As I was lying there with my eyes closed, resting, I could hear all the noise around me, and when I heard Chris and Bobby pull up, I was surprised to see them. I thought I was behind them all day. We chatted a moment and then I decided I should probably get moving.

It was another long, slow climb with lots of walking because the trail was very steep and rocky. I finally made it to the top and then the descent was also steep and rocky. I had to ride the brakes all the way down. A rider in front of me dropped his sleeping pad on the trail so I picked it up. When I passed him on the descent and gave him the sleeping pad, he said he thought it must have bounced right off the bike because the trail was so rocky.

I pulled over to take a break and rest my hands. I was braking so much on the descent, they were starting to hurt. I thought I should probably eat also, since with the heat, I hadn't had anything since breakfast in Ovando. I kept moving down the trail and saw the Llama House Hostel. I took another break and chatted with some riders. The Llama House seemed very lovely, with great hosts, many camping spots, and even a couple of snacks, but with about 15-plus other cyclists there, it seemed like the wrong place to stay for the night if I wanted to get moving early in the morning. It was also a little too early for me to stop for the day; the sun hadn't even set yet and I was still dreaming of the hotel.

Just as I was getting ready to go, Erik, Gyorgy and Joe came in and completely caught me off guard. I had assumed they were ahead of me all day, too. They had stayed at Seeley Lake when it was raining and went to town for steak before camping out. They are great guys and I was very excited to see them again.

Chris and Bobby were getting ready to leave the Llama House because they wanted to hit 100 miles for the day. They were going to camp about 20 miles up the road and suggested the rest of us camp with them, but I wanted that hotel and thought I would be able to make it by around midnight, so I was going to push on. The rest of us decided to stick together through the night even after I reminded them how much slower I was than they were. When I decided to do the ride, I knew I'd be alone most of the time, but it was nice to meet such kind people who were willing to slow down a little for one evening.

We started up the climb, riding slowly and sometimes pushing our bikes. I would stop and say, "Sorry, but I have to push for a bit," and they all said, "So do we." It was so cute, and I would smile and think, *Sure*. As the night got darker, we started to hit cold pockets through rolling areas. Since we were all together, if one person needed to stop to put on a jacket, we would all stop.

Then, it would get warm, and we would take off our jackets. It was slow going, and I felt like it was all my fault, because of how slowly I ride. The clock kept ticking later and later, and getting to Helena, Montana, for the hotel was starting to seem out of the question. I was slowing everyone down and starting to feel really tired; I felt so much pressure to keep up with everyone.

We decided to stop one last time and put on more clothes. As I stood waiting for the others, I tripped over my bike and landed right on top of it, with the drive chain on the ground. I was so upset when I realized I had bent my derailleur hanger, which meant changing gears was now an issue. I was trying to make some micro-adjustments, but I was getting frustrated and embarrassed, and it was dark and cold. I just said, "It's broken; let's keep going."

I felt awful, holding everyone up and now biking even slower. I told them to ride ahead, and they all declined. I found a gear that was working and just kept going, trying to remember to not shift gears. We kept riding, and it was dark with a lot of weird rocks and divots and the next thing I know, I'm on the ground. I somehow crashed my bike and hit my head. Everyone came over to check on me and we took a minute to look over my helmet and make sure I was okay. I was very embarrassed, but everyone was so kind. Erik kept checking in on me, telling me his wife was a nurse and he wanted to make sure I didn't have a concussion.

I thought I might have lost sight of the road but I'm pretty sure I just fell asleep. It was all a blur at 1 a.m. I just kept thinking this was not my night. I was just trying to hold it together and not cry in front of everyone. First, I couldn't shift and now I crashed my bike, but I had to keep riding. Eventually, we made it to Helena. We started calling hotels, but it was now after 3 a.m. Finally, we found a room on the other side of town.

We started our way up the road and arrived just before 4 a.m. All I wanted to do was get into a room and sleep away this day. I was exhausted, embarrassed and just needed to be alone. When we got into the room, it hadn't been cleaned—this was our luck. We returned to the desk to get a new room, and the same thing happened with the second room. At this point, we were all very frustrated; it felt like someone was playing a joke on us. None of us were in the mood for this. We got a third room, and it was clean. It was almost 5 a.m. by this time, so I showered and got right to bed. As I crawled into bed after a nice, hot shower, I thought, *This wasn't the best decision to ride all night, but I'm glad I had friends with me,* and I was sound asleep within minutes.

June 14: Informal camping in Ovando, MT, to Helena, MT
Route Mileage: 277.45 – 376.79
Distance: 99.34 miles
Elevation Gain: 10,804 feet

Make the Best of a Bad Situation

Day 5 After sleeping for three hours, I quietly packed up my bike and sneaked out of the hotel room. Still exhausted, I headed outside to work on the bike. I wanted to fix the bike on my own to prove to myself that I could do it. I messed around with the bike for a while, wasting time and getting frustrated, but I finally got the derailleur hanger switched out and I could change gears again. While I was happy that I did it, I figured I would swing by the local bike shop to have the bike looked over more thoroughly. After a couple hundred miles of riding and a little crash, I thought it best to ensure I hadn't missed anything.

I headed over to the Great Divide Cyclery and Garage where they looked over the bike and said it was all good except the brake pads could use a refresh, and they quickly switched them out for me. The service was terrific; the people were super-kind and great to work with. With the bike back to normal, I headed downtown and found a place to get lunch.

I grabbed some burritos, one for lunch and one for dinner that night, and felt like I could finally start my day. Aaron had told me it would be hot for the climb out of Helena as it has no tree cover and that I didn't want to do this climb in the afternoon, even though that was when I had to do it.

As I was leaving Helena just before 1 p.m., I wasn't optimistic about how my day would go with so much climbing ahead of me during the hottest part of the day. The climb out of Helena was long and the sun was intense. I stopped anywhere I could find shade for a quick break and tried to make as much forward progress as possible, even if that meant pushing the bike.

The tiniest stream was flowing next to the road, and I stopped and splashed some water on myself to cool down. About halfway up, I ran into other cyclists all gathered in a huge patch of shade. I stopped to sit down and eat a small snack, but really, I was just trying to take advantage of that shade. I kept pushing up the climb, thinking: *The sun will set at some point. Then it will cool off and then I can get some more miles in. I need more miles.*

When I made it near the top, I started on that second burrito and it tasted so good, still warm from the hot day. After finishing it, I started down the Lava Mountain trail section. The trail reminded me of so many sections on the Superior Hiking Trail. It was rough, rocky and rooty, so pushing my heavy bike through this was very difficult. There were some bikeable sections, but after a while, I was too tired, so it became a hike-a-bike section for me. I thought, *How am I only on the fifth day out here and already feeling this exhausted? I still have 20 days left*, but I couldn't think about that because I needed to focus on making it through this moment.

I finally reached the end of Lava Mountain and descended into Basin, Montana, on a nice gravel road, where I found lots of riders outside the community center. It was a relief to make it to town, and I again could not wait to sleep. The bar next door had pizza and soda, so I was able to get some food.

I ate dinner with my new friends and as we finished, Gyorgy, Erik and Joe chatted about how they had all been riding together, off and on, for the past couple of days but that they would need to split up starting the next morning as they all had different goals and paces. I hadn't really been riding with them as much as catching them at the end of the day, so it just meant I might not be seeing them as much. It was nice to get to know them, and I was hopeful we would stay friends.

I headed back to my bike to lay out my bivy, feeling disappointed that I didn't even ride 40 miles for the day and now had to figure out how to make up 60 miles over the next 20 days. That thought alone exhausted my brain. But I was also smiling because the day had seemed like a bust, but I had made some friends, which was a huge win.

June 15: Helena, MT, to informal camping in Basin, MT
Route Mileage: 376.79 – 414.33
Distance: 37.54 miles
Elevation Gain: 5,413 feet

Take a Moment to Relax

Day 6 There were people sleeping everywhere so there was no snoozing my alarm. I had left some items inside the community center to charge overnight, so I tiptoed inside to grab my things, trying not to wake up anyone. I left town right away, hoping that would give me more time to get my miles in for the day. After about 10 miles, I had warmed up so I stopped to cook some oatmeal and coffee. The sun was shining and warmed my body as I took in the landscape around me. I sat on a gravel road, enjoying the moment and relaxing my body and mind for the day ahead.

As I sat eating my oatmeal, I thought about the amazing places I had traveled so far and how things were going, both the ups and downs of the last five days. I started to realize that I was usually the last rider riding at the night's end and the first to leave every day. I felt like I was riding more hours to get the same miles as the people around me and it was exhausting, but it had become my way of riding and the only way to get the miles I wanted.

After a little food, the riding into Butte, Montana, was great, making it an enjoyable morning with the sun shining and the tolerable climbs. But as I approached Butte, I was ready for lunch. I ran into Erik and Gyorgy, and we grabbed some lunch at a taco place where I took a burrito for dinner, too. Erik took off, and Gyorgy took a half-day break. I was sad he wouldn't keep going with us that afternoon, but I knew he needed to do what was best for him.

With a quick stop at a gas station for snacks, I was ready for the afternoon as I started the climb out of Butte. The climb was nice and when I reached the top, the road opened up to a wide valley with the most fantastic view. I could see rolling roads going across the valley through high trees and an open sky for miles. The riding was perfect. Everything was going perfectly, until I hit Fleecer Ridge.

Fleecer Ridge was different from what I expected. You can see the trail in several films and it doesn't look that bad. But when I started going down the trail it was steeper than I had imagined. I knew I would be walking my bike but didn't realize how hard that would be. My bike wanted to go faster than I could move. Loose rocks covered the trail, and navigating my footing was challenging. It was so steep I had to be careful not to slip or drop my bike. I was laughing and crying, not sure how I felt about the situation. It didn't take long to descend, but it felt like hours. I was so glad I made it to the bottom right before dark, or it would have been a lot more difficult.

I got back on my bike and started down the road. I thought riding at night would get easier as the days went on, but that wasn't the case on this night. As I was heading into Wise River, Montana, I was feeling tired and having a hard time concentrating. I realized I hadn't eaten my burrito or had any other food since lunch. I also couldn't catch up on sleep and was increasingly more tired every day. I tried eating the burrito I had carried all day, but at this point, I was so tired and overly hungry, I was starting to get a stomachache. I would take a bite, and it would take me 10 minutes to chew. After a couple more bites, I couldn't take any more. But I needed something to stay awake, so I stuck with my go-to snack: peach rings. You can't go wrong with some peach rings.

I finally passed through the town of Wise River and turned down the paved road in search of a campground I had seen on the map about 10 miles up the road from town. I kept pedaling down the quiet road, past midnight now, and I was freaked out when I noticed eyes in the woods. *More mountain lions staring me down?* I wondered, as I turned off the light on my helmet and used my bike-mounted light to avoid looking around and seeing anything else. I couldn't tell if I was seeing eyes or if it was in my head after a while because I thought I saw so many.

I was tired and biking those 10 miles, even on a flat paved road, felt like it might take all night, but I finally made it to the campground around 1:30 a.m. and was relieved to be done for the day. As I crawled into my bivy, I thought about the day I had had: the most beautiful landscapes, more wildlife sightings, and time to relax and reset for the big-mile day I needed. Although I was still feeling a little nervous, given all the eyes I had been seeing, that didn't keep me awake. Not much could have.

June 16: Informal camping in Basin, MT, to Pettengill Campground north of Wise River, MT
Route Mileage: 414.33 – 512.53
Distance: 98.20 miles
Elevation Gain: 12,359 feet

There's Something Special about Home

Day 7 I decided to wake up with the sun because I needed some extra sleep after the late night. I packed up the bike, and as I was returning to the road, I saw Erik camping just 50 yards away. It was nice to say good morning before I hit the road.

The morning air was cool and I had a nice, steady climb on a paved road to start my day. As I started up the climb, I couldn't believe I was actually riding my bike. I hardly had to walk, which was a first. It felt amazing. Erik passed me on the way up, but I reached the top of the climb just a little after him. We saw some lodges on the map after the descent, and we both wanted to find a place to have breakfast so we rode together. The descent was fast and fun but also went by way too quickly. I rode behind Erik and enjoyed the fast pace for once because we were on a paved road where I felt much more comfortable and could actually look around. While I still had to be mindful that I was on a bike, it was a nice break from how I had been riding for the last few days.

When we saw the Grasshopper Inn, I was eager to get breakfast there. The staff told us it was a Bed and Breakfast but said they could serve us breakfast if we paid cash. I carried a little cash the entire trip just in case I ever needed it, and I happily agreed because not only is breakfast my favorite meal of the day, I really wanted some real coffee! I sat and enjoyed the food as I looked over the maps for the day. After breakfast, Erik and I parted ways, which was always good and bad. I was out here to ride alone, but it was also nice to have company sometimes.

Leaving the Grasshopper Inn, it was already getting hot as I started down a long, flat section. I was so confused by the weather in Montana. I thought it would be cool and get hot later in the trip, but that was not the case. With little shade in this area, it made for a long afternoon. While I knew I was making progress, I felt like I wasn't even moving at times. I was hitting a low.

I turned on the Divide playlist the kids had created for me before I left. It was nice to hear the songs they had picked, even Joey's choice of "Around the World," which played for seven minutes and made me laugh. I never knew that song was so long. I switched to the "Trolls" soundtrack, which Molly had picked, and listened to "Get Back Up Again." As I listened to the words, it was like the song was describing how I felt so many moments of the day. I thought, *This will be the theme song to my ride and if I need a pick-me-up, I'll listen to it.* As I continued down the paved road, listening a second time, crying now, and then a third time, I thought, *You can do this, Mary, keep pedaling.*

I checked my phone and I had cell reception. Instead of calling home, I decided it was time to send some postcards; plus, I was looking for any reason to take a break. I had found an app before my trip where I could upload my phone pictures, and it would create a postcard and send it wherever I wanted. I scrolled through my phone, found some fun pictures, and started sending postcards home and I felt much better. It was a challenging afternoon, and these small things that reminded me of home really lifted my mood.

I looked at my miles for the day, and there was some hope that I might go well over the 100 miles I needed. That was exciting!

As the sun went down, I started to see a glow from the town in the distance, but I was ready to camp now, and those last miles at night were so hard. I realized I was too close to town to stop, but it was getting late and I was tired. Frustrated that I had to keep going when all I wanted to do was sleep, I kept cycling down the road.

I had cell reception again, so I called home and chatted with Aaron. It was nice to have a little distraction to keep my mind off wanting to sleep and he was always so positive. He told me about how things were going at home: the kids were spending time with their cousins, he was working at the bike shop, and everyone was happy, which made me a little sad because I wasn't there but also happy to know they were having fun while I was out here, having fun or something in that realm.

When we hung up, I still had a couple more miles to go, so I started eating salted nut rolls and peach rings non-stop, just trying to keep myself alert enough to make it to town. I made it into Lima, Montana, and found Erik in the campground. I joked that it seemed like he couldn't lose me, and we laughed. I wanted to get a motel room, but Erik told me all the rooms were booked, so we camped out behind the building. I set up camp and was happy to have a friend with me as this was an interesting little campground.

June 17: North of Wise River, MT, to informal camping in Lima, MT

Route Mileage: 512.53 – 638.17

Distance: 125.64 miles

Elevation Gain: 8,215 feet

Food is Energy

Day 8 Waking up behind a motel was all the motivation I needed to get moving; I didn't want to be there any longer than I had to be. I swung by a gas station on my way out of town, but finding food first thing in the morning was challenging because I wasn't hungry. I was still tired and didn't know what I wanted to eat now or what I would want to eat eight hours from now. But I needed food, so I grabbed pastries, rice crispy bars, and some OJ. Erik and I rode together for about 15 miles and stopped at a beautiful lake to eat breakfast and have coffee. As we finished eating and filtering water, I told Erik to take off, that he didn't need to ride slowly with me today.

Montana couldn't help but give us another hot day, and while the terrain was very rideable with no real climbs, the lack of climbing almost seemed more difficult because all I needed to do was ride my bike, but that was the one thing I didn't want to do. I was constantly stopping and rearranging my shorts and I couldn't get comfortable. My butt hurt, and I found myself pushing my bike for no reason other than I didn't feel like cycling. I tried taking my shorts off and wearing my leggings, then slipping back into my shorts when that didn't fix it.

I was trying to figure out if it was pain or discomfort. Or was I just tired? I kept trucking along, taking naps in any shade I could find and trying to find something positive, but that was difficult when my brain was just focused on how hard this was at this moment. The scenery didn't change as I rode across a valley from one range to the next. The day felt tedious and lengthy, and I was irritated because I was moving so slowly when I should have been cycling faster.

It was a mentally challenging day, and I knew I needed to get out of this mood, but I wasn't sure how. I remembered a training ride when it felt like everything went wrong: the bike didn't feel right, my leg hurt, I was tired and hungry, and I didn't bring enough food for the 100-mile ride. I ended up calling for a ride because, although I didn't want to give up on my training ride, I needed to figure out what was going wrong so that if this happened during the Divide, I could fix it. This was that day when nothing felt right, and I needed to fix it. Even though I was tired and irritated, I thought I could turn this around.

I sat down on the side of the road and decided it was time to make some ramen noodles. As I warmed the water, I tried to focus on changing my attitude. I drank the warm, salty broth and started feeling better. I knew it was only a few hours until Island Park, Idaho, but I needed some food now to make sure I could get there. I continued down the road, with my body and my mind feeling better. I would make it to Island Park soon. I could do this.

I finally arrived in Island Park, where I hoped to get some food. I headed over to the local restaurant for dinner and then stopped for some groceries, all before 9 p.m., which felt like a huge win. I got a call from a rider who said I could share a room if I wanted to sleep on the floor. I was so thankful to be able to rinse my shorts because they were causing me serious discomfort and I thought that rinsing them out might help. I squeezed into the very small room with three bikes, took a quick shower and headed right to bed. It was before 11 p.m., an early night for me, but I was so happy after that long day. I fell asleep thinking, *I have just entered Idaho!* It was the second of five states and leaving Montana behind me felt amazing.

June 18: Informal camping in Lima, MT, to Island Park, ID

Route Mileage: 638.17 – 724.48

Distance: 86.31 miles

Elevation Gain: 3,428 feet

Idaho

Friends can be Made When You Least Expect It

Day 9 Sharing a room can pose challenges. We all had so much riding ahead of us, but I needed to get going as early as possible every day. I couldn't afford to waste any daylight because cycling in the dark was not going well. So I tried to be respectful and wake up with everyone else. Within minutes of everyone's alarms going off, I popped out of bed and was right back to biking. I knew they would pass me in a couple of hours, anyway, and I needed that extra time.

The road was great heading out of Island Park, and I was excited that I would be in and out of Idaho in one day. I stopped at a gas station mid-morning for a hot coffee and a new toothbrush since I had dropped mine. With all the candy I was eating, I really needed to brush my teeth. Since I had cell reception, I took the opportunity to call home also. After a little extra sleep the night before and a phone call to the family, I was in a great mood. I just knew it was going to be a good day.

While I was drinking my coffee, a touring cyclist came over and started chatting with me, which was a bonus pick-me-up for the morning. He was a friendly guy who was touring the Trans Am. We were by an ATM and he asked if I needed money, saying, "I can get you cash. I have everything back home paid for, so if you need anything...." I turned him down, but it was a kind gesture and another reminder of how great the cycling community is and how many cyclists are willing to help each other out.

I was close to Yellowstone National Park, so there was a lot of traffic on a short road section before heading back onto gravel. As I pedaled down this busy road, I realized for the first time how much I liked gravel roads. I turned back down onto a gravel trail and I thought, *I like gravel but not this kind of gravel.* Trying to keep my bike upright as I kept losing traction in the deep, loose, sandy gravel, I managed to fall over several times, which was embarrassing even if no one saw me. I thought, *How is it possible to be so embarrassed when you're all alone?* One of the times I fell, I spilled my Chex Mix. I was annoyed because it was one of my few snacks for the day, so I had to sit and pick it all up. I put the Chex back into the bag, one Chex piece at a time. Just as I was almost done, Chris and Bobby came by, and we all laughed. Now, I was even more embarrassed. As I ate the Chex Mix the rest of the day, I ate gravel bits too, which was gross, but food is food on the Divide, which made me laugh.

Finally, I got onto a trail that was absolutely amazing. Winding high over the river on my left and an old train tunnel on my right, it was like a movie moment. I took a little break to look out over the river with the full forest and enjoy this beautiful spot. As I continued down the trail, I crossed the Warm River, and I started climbing again. It was a steep road climb with a narrow shoulder, but it was short, and I just pushed through it and got it done.

As I neared the top, it opened up to the most magnificent greens with the Grand Tetons in the background. What a moment! As I stood and stared out across the valley, I couldn't believe how far I'd come. I'd crossed an entire state and had ridden almost 800 miles. I thought, *What a huge accomplishment already and I still have so much riding ahead of me.* I kept riding down the road, distracted by the amazing place I was in when I stumbled upon Squirrel Creek

Ranch. I parked my bike outside, and I saw another bike, one I hadn't seen before. I walked into the restaurant and met Audrey, another woman who was riding the Divide. Excited to have met another female rider, we ate lunch together and decided to leave Squirrel Creek Ranch at the same time and ride together.

As we rode down the trail, we talked, laughed and pushed each other through the rolling hills. We had so much in common yet also many differences, and I immediately knew we would be friends. She was a fantastic cyclist and brought me so much joy. She was able to push me to ride a little harder than I normally do. It was almost like I wanted to prove I could keep up with her, even though I knew I had nothing to prove. We both just wanted to be out, riding our bikes and doing our best. We crossed from Idaho into Wyoming and snapped a border crossing photo, as I thought, *One more state down.*

As we got near Flagg Ranch, the sun was setting, and I wanted to keep going but she was ready to call it a day, so we exchanged numbers, hoping to meet up the next day at Colter Bay. I was emotional riding away because the experience of meeting another woman doing the same thing as me was so meaningful. I could connect with her in ways I couldn't with the other riders. I started to believe a little more that I could do this.

I headed toward Colter Bay, where I planned to camp. As I crossed the river, the sun was in a perfect space behind the trees for a fantastic sunset that silhouetted the mountains. As I climbed up the road, I slowly watched the sky turn from a purple-pink to a dark black, filled with stars. In these moments with the sky filled with twinkling stars so different from the city, I felt lucky.

Just as I made it to Colter Bay, it started drizzling. I was tired and couldn't figure out where the campground was. Frustrated and getting wet, I decided I would keep riding; after all, it was only 10 p.m. I saw there was supposed to be another campground a little way up the road so I looked for that one. I kept moving up the route, but I couldn't find that one either, so I just kept cycling down this windy highway with cars flying by every couple of minutes until I could find somewhere to sleep.

Finally, I turned off the highway and saw parking lots filled with cars and people camping along the road. I had seen a message from Erik that he was camped off this road, so I kept going in hopes of finding him, but then I lost cell reception. It was just after 1 a.m. and I was exhausted, so instead of finding Erik, I found a safe place to tuck in between a couple of car-campers. I got into my sleeping bag, so happy to be in bed. I checked for cell reception one more time, but I didn't have any, which meant I wasn't going to be able to get a hold of Audrey or Erik the next day, and that was a huge bummer.

June 19: Island Park, ID, to south of Turpin Meadow Campground, WY

Route Mileage: 724.48 – 843.39

Distance: 118.91 miles

Elevation Gain: 7,828 feet

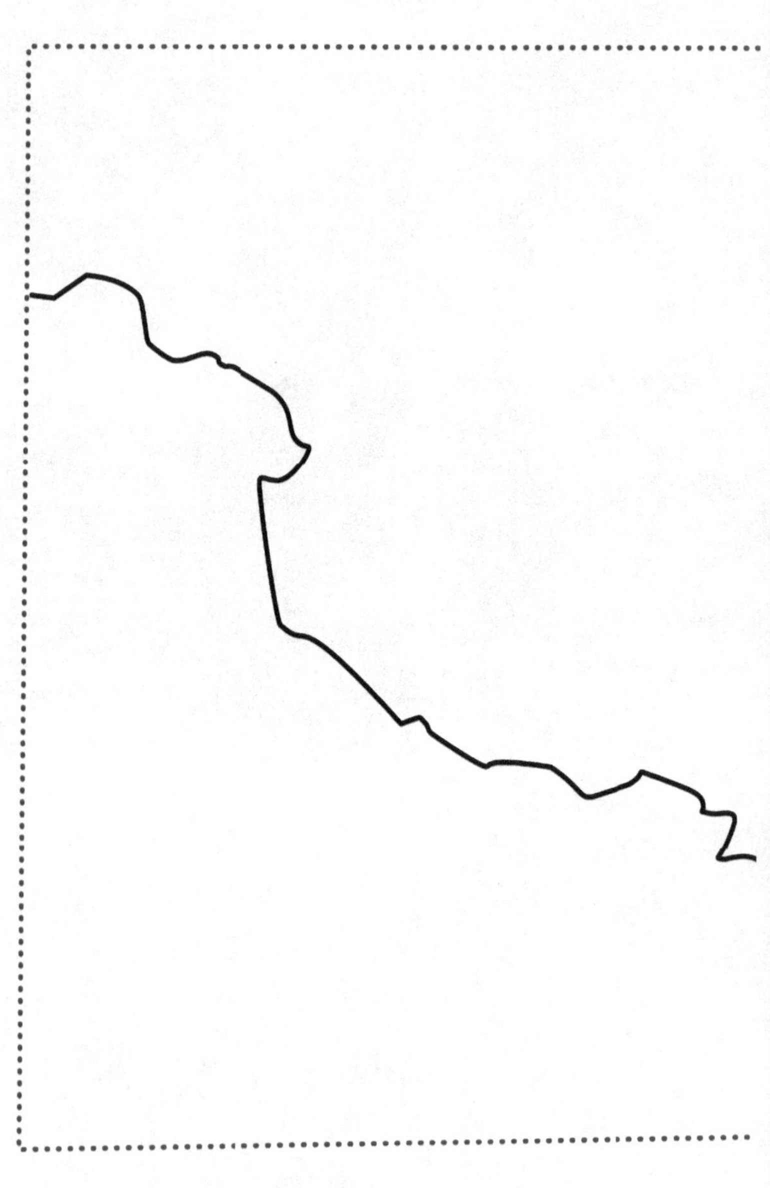

Wyoming

You're Never Too Old

Day 10 Waking up, I didn't want to snooze my alarm because there were people so close by and I would feel terrible if I woke them. I quickly and quietly returned to the road, trying not to disturb anyone. As I approached Turpin Meadow Ranch, I was hoping to get breakfast, but it was closed for a private event. Frustrated, I kept pedaling up the road where there was a lodge.

Up the climb, I was actually *riding* my bike. I realized that climbing in the morning was getting way more manageable and even enjoyable. I didn't know who this new Mary was who liked climbing, but I loved her. As I reached the top of the climb, I saw Togwotee Mountain Lodge. I was so happy at the thought of breakfast, but when I got inside, the restaurant was closed because of short staffing.

The lodge had some hot coffee and packaged pastries for hotel guests, so I bought those and that was breakfast. I grabbed a bunch of sugar packets and creamer and made some "breakfast shots," a bikepacking tradition our friend had taught me on our Florida ride. So many memories flooded back: swimming in the ocean, camping out on the beach, and the cops waking us up in the middle of the night because we had camped out in a public pavilion.

It was a good reminder of one of the reasons I love bikepacking: learning to make the best of the situation.

While relaxing on the lodge's porch, drinking my hot coffee, I met a rider looking for breakfast who was also disappointed the restaurant was closed. I chatted with him for a moment before I packed up my stuff in hopes of finding a restaurant for lunch. I really wanted some food fresh from a kitchen, not from plastic.

The riding for the rest of the morning was great, with some road sections that made for nice breaks. Climbing up Togwotee Pass, I was really excited when I got to the top where the Trans Am and Divide cross paths. I stood there, looking out over the valley, knowing so many cyclists pass this spot going both north and south on the Divide or east and west on the Trans Am.

Just as I made it over the pass, I got a nice descent into a small town where I was going to try to get lunch. There were not many cars outside the lodge so I was nervous it might be closed, but when I walked in, the restaurant was open. I found a spot at the bar and was so happy to sit down for a bit. Using the lodge wifi, I was able to check my phone and saw that I had a message from Erik. He had let me know he had to stop because of a family matter, and I was even more bummed that I didn't get to see him the night before. I thought, *I really hope we stay friends*.

I saw the rider from that morning also sitting at the bar so we chatted over lunch. I enjoyed an entire pepperoni pizza while talking to this very kind man with lots of bikepacking experience to share. This was his fourth time on the Divide and he was in his 70s, which is very inspiring. I couldn't believe someone would attempt this ride four times during their retirement. I was struggling every day and I was half his age.

After lunch, I headed up the climb for Union Pass, which was long and hard with three big humps, not like a mountain pass, but huge hills I had to get over. The riding was challenging but the view was amazing when I looked out over the mountainside as the sun set.

By the time I was done climbing, it was late and I was tired. It was always late, and I was always tired. After 10 days, I thought I would be used to this, but I wasn't yet. I still had my 100-mile-per-day goal and today, I wasn't even close, so I needed to ride as late as possible.

It was just after 9 p.m. and I was starting to feel like I needed to stop when I ran into a northbound cyclist who told me about a warming shelter and gave me its approximate location. I looked over the map and counted the miles to the shelter, hoping I could make it there. It was a good goal to focus on so that I could keep pushing into the night. But as I was riding, I kept getting confused and reversing the numbers of how far I thought I had to go. Then I started to get so sleepy that I thought I had miscalculated the distance and missed the shelter all together, or maybe it was still so far away? I was so confused. So, I found a spot to camp. As I lay in my bivy, looking over the map from the day's ride, I thought: *From the start of the day to the end, what a great day it has been. Two cups of hot coffee, pizza for lunch with an inspiring man, and mesmerizing views.*

June 20: South of Turpin Meadow Campground, WY, to informal campground (right before warming house), WY

Route Mileage: 843.39 – 912.05

Distance: 68.66 miles

Elevation Gain: 9,544 feet

Be Flexible

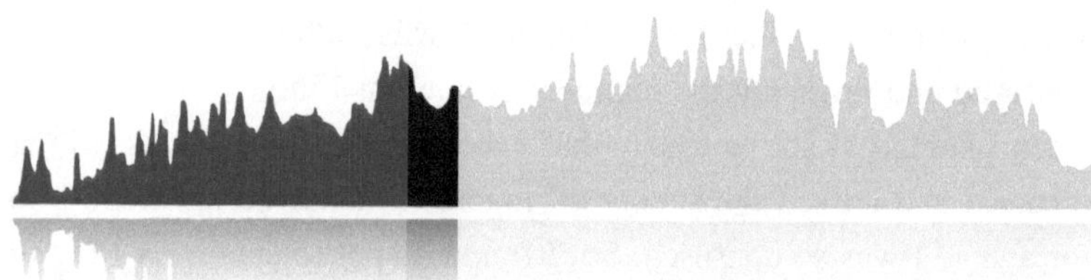

Day 11 I couldn't believe it the next morning when, within a mile, I found the shelter I had been looking for the night before. At first, I was annoyed that I had been so close, but then I realized it was probably best that I had just camped where I did. Usually, I headed to bed so late and got up so early that a shared space wasn't ideal.

As morning pressed on, I stopped by the side of the road to look over the map, thinking about how the day would go, and I fell asleep in the warm sun. I woke up a little confused and very tired. I started to look over the map again when I noticed I was going to get to the city of Pinedale, Wyoming, by lunch time. I felt disappointed because it was a large town, right on the route, and it would have been a great place to get a hotel room. But me and hotels didn't seem to line up very well so it would just have to be another night of camping.

I kept moving down the road with a little climbing and then a gradual descent into town. I made it almost 60 miles by noon. I was so stoked! As I cycled down the main street of Pinedale, I found a diner so I could have breakfast, even though it was lunchtime. I ordered a massive plate of pancakes, hot coffee, a Coke with no ice and a Gatorade; I was so excited.

After ordering, I went back outside to lay out my camp gear to dry. I sat and reviewed my cue cards while I waited for my food when I realized I was onto ACA map 3. I was done with my first cue card! I couldn't believe I was almost 1,000 miles into this ride! I thought, *No wonder I am so drained all the time*.

The sun was shining, and my gear was getting nice and dry, but the sun also made me sleepy. I thought about getting a room and just taking a half-day off. I tried convincing myself that I was too sleepy to keep riding and needed to rest before going into the Great Divide Basin. I really just wanted any excuse to take a break.

I called and chatted with Aaron, and told him I might get a room, but after talking, all of sudden I wasn't so sure that was a good idea. It just isn't my style, and I realized I needed to keep going, which meant no hotel room for me. I knew I would be so mad if I stopped for the day at 1 p.m. and wasted all that daylight. Plus, the weather was excellent, and I was heading into the Great Divide Basin, where the weather can make or break your day. Headwinds in the high desert can be the enemy, and rain can turn the roads into mud, slowing you down and turning one or two days of riding into three.

I finished lunch, packed up my gear and started moving toward the Basin. Just 10 miles up the road in Boulder, Wyoming, there was another gas station, so I stopped again for a little more food and Gatorade. During those 10 miles I hadn't felt that great, maybe because of the hot sun or the full belly, so I took a quick nap on a bench outside the gas station. I was happy with the miles I had completed to this point in the day, but needed to listen to my body so that I could make good progress into the evening. As much as I wanted to keep pushing hard, I knew a little nap could be really good for my body and mind.

I was feeling better as my food settled so I left Boulder and started my ride into the Great Divide Basin. As I started down the road, it was wide open with no wind, and I felt like I was flying through the miles. With a clear blue sky and no clouds in sight, I kept looking around and thinking, *How lucky I am to be here right now.*

The Basin was shockingly gorgeous—wide open, high desert with no trees—and so different from anything I had seen up to this point. Even though it is relatively flat, it felt different than the long stretch out of Lima. This time, I was ready for flat, which made a huge difference going into it. The rolling roads and lack of wind made for a fun evening. As the sun set, the sky stayed clear and I was able to see the most fantastic starry night. This is what I love: the clear sky with so many stars. You can't see that in the city.

I took Aaron's advice and kept riding as late as possible because when the riding is good, you don't stop, especially in the Great Divide Basin, because you never know what the wind will do the next day. I kept riding until after midnight and enjoyed every moment: the calm; the cooler weather as the sun went down; the dark, clear sky; and the vast, open ranch land.

I picked a spot to camp and as I lay in my bivy and stared at the starry sky, I thought about how cool it was that I got to sleep out in the open, with no tree cover. I had thought it might be scary, being in the wide open, but it was beautiful and relaxing. As I looked up at the amazing stars, I didn't *want* to sleep as much as I knew I *had* to.

June 21: Informal campground, WY, to the Great Divide Basin (informal camping outside of Atlantic City, WY)

Route Mileage: 912.05 – 1034.90

Distance: 122.85 miles

Elevation Gain: 5,620 feet

Remember to Smile

Day 12 Still tired and groggy, I slept so hard that I snoozed the alarm several times without even noticing. Within minutes of waking up, I managed to crush my glasses. I was so upset; I couldn't believe I had broken them. I must have forgotten to put my glasses away the night before, and they ended up under my sleeping pad. I cracked the frame at the nose bridge.

I carried disposable contacts in case of an emergency because I don't see well without my glasses. The contacts make me really sleepy no matter the time of day and were less than ideal to use at night because of all the dust and dirt on my hands. I had my prescription sunglasses for the daytime at least, so I could make do.

I packed up the bike, trying not to focus too much on what had happened because there was nothing I could do about it now, put on my sunglasses and headed for Atlantic City, Wyoming. I planned to stop at a restaurant for breakfast and thought I would have to figure out a plan to fix my glasses there.

Just before Atlantic City, I passed a rest area and stopped to fill up my water bottles. I thought I should see if there was anything I could do about the glasses before heading back into the desert, so I tried the tube patch kit glue, but that didn't work. A man saw me working on my glasses and brought over some super glue. It looked like it might hold, so I put them in the case and was back to riding.

I arrived in Atlantic City and was surprised by the tiny town, way smaller than I imagined, with a population of fewer than 60. I found the little restaurant, but now I was nervous to go inside in this super-small town. There weren't any customers when I went in, but the server told me to sit wherever I would like, so I found a table and immediately pulled out my glasses. The super glue hadn't worked, probably because I was in a hurry to leave, and hadn't given it time to dry before the glasses got rattled around in their case on my ride to town. I was starting to lose hope of fixing my glasses and getting very anxious about using the contacts.

I ordered some breakfast and was looking for something to take for later when the restaurant owner recommended a giant breakfast burrito filled with egg, cheese, ham and bacon. It sounded perfect. While I sat there, looking like a lost puppy, the owner noticed I was trying to fix my glasses. She asked how she could help while I waited for my food. I asked if she knew anywhere in town I could find some glue, and she said no but started looking around the restaurant. I put some repair tape on to see if that would hold, but it wasn't working. Then she came back with what she called "ancient" super glue, and to the surprise of both of us, it was still liquid.

We applied the glue and it dried quickly and held. Smiling ear to ear, my attitude quickly changed from disappointed to cheerful. After it completely dried, I applied the fabric repair tape over the bridge and crossed my fingers that between the two, the glasses would make it to the end. I finished breakfast, packed the bike and returned to the Basin, so grateful for her kindness.

The climb out of Atlantic City was hard, especially in the heat of the morning. It only seemed to get hotter all day in the Basin. I needed to carry a lot of water, and I had to manage how much I was drinking because it would be almost 100 miles before I could get more. Not wanting to filter water at the well in the Basin, I carried a couple more water bottles on the bike, tucking them anywhere they would fit. I used a foldable backpack for the extra water and food, which gave me the additional carrying capacity to be confident if something were to happen and I couldn't get out of the Basin the next day. More water is always better when you're in the sun.

As I pedaled through the Basin, the landscape was exceptional. You could see for miles with a low brush cover over the ground. Then I saw wild horses for the first time—it was so stunning to see them run through the ranch land, free with no boundaries.

The day was hot and the shade was nowhere, until some clouds appeared for about an hour in the afternoon. I tried to take advantage by quickly pedaling ahead of the clouds and then stopping to eat while the clouds were over me. The timing was tricky but well worth the effort for a bit of shade. The burrito was terrific because it had stayed warm in the hot sun all morning in my foldable backpack.

The rest of the afternoon was still hot, and I began realizing that managing my water was more challenging than I had anticipated. I wanted to drink more water, but I also knew I needed to be smart and save some for the next day.

Looking out into the desert as the sun was setting, I saw that the sunset was, again, perfect, with the sky glowing orange. Once dark, the sky filled with so many stars again and the stillness of the desert was calming. I was hoping to make it out of the Great Divide Basin and into Rawlins, Wyoming, for a hotel, but I was too slow and tired to cover the extra 40 miles at the night's end, so I picked a spot and got ready for bed.

As I was tucking myself in, I remembered how I had broken my glasses that morning and that I'd better put them away safely. They were working perfectly, which reminded me that sometimes a small gesture from a stranger can make the most significant difference in your day when you're having a rough moment.

June 22: Informal camping outside Atlantic City, WY, to informal camping between Atlantic City and Rawlins, WY

Route Mileage: 1034.90 – 1136.44

Distance: 101.54 miles

Elevation Gain: 7,047 feet

Enjoy the Little Moments

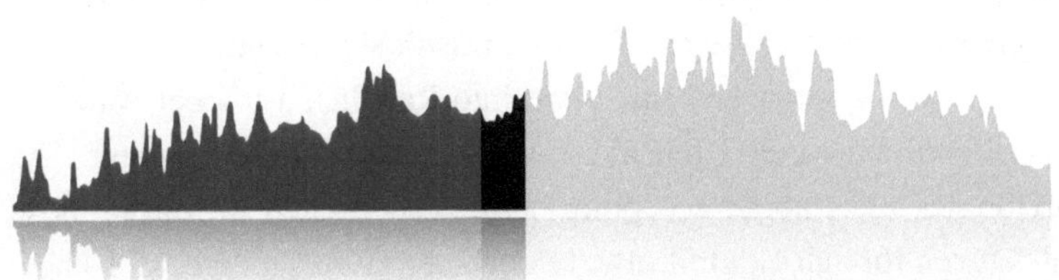

Day 13 Waking up, I immediately felt sad that I was missing Joey's birthday as it's one of my favorite days of the year. I knew he would have a fun day at home, but I couldn't help but feel jealous that I wasn't there with him.

I was very emotional about missing Joey's birthday, but I still had biking to do, so I needed to focus on that. I was hoping for some big miles so I could make it to Brush Mountain Lodge for a room and to clean up, and I hoped that would distract me. Aaron had raved about how wonderful Brush was, and I wanted to see what it was all about.

I had heard that it's a special place for Divide riders. Not only because it's about halfway on the route, but the owner opens her doors for everyone, no matter when you arrive. She has extra supplies, like bear spray or sunscreen left by other riders. She offers food to riders and only asks for donations, a pay-what-you-can type of program. With half-price rooms for cyclists, it's really a nice place to look forward to. I'd been told the people at Brush really care about the riders, and that's special when you're alone for so long.

I had ended up camping about 3-5 miles from a 40-mile paved road that took me into Rawlins. I got lucky that I stopped when I did, because the camping was limited once I hit that pavement. I was not expecting pavement, so that was a pleasant little surprise and an easy start to my day. I spent the morning finishing the Basin and was looking forward to lunch in Rawlins and getting more water, even though I had rationed my water well. I was down to the last of six water bottles I had started with the day before and I had just enough to get to Rawlins. The road was quiet most of the morning, which was great because the shoulder wasn't significant.

As I approached the climb into Rawlins, a trucker came by and offered me water. I felt like I was in a bit of a predicament. The Divide has rules about accepting help and I wanted to follow those rules, even though I didn't always consider myself a "racer." I knew that when I looked back at the ride, I wanted to know I completed it the same as everyone else. Since I hadn't stopped the man or asked for anything, I felt this situation fell under the Trail Angel/Magic rule: an individual(s) who offers gifts along the trail without being solicited. Plus, I knew I had enough water to make it to town, so he wasn't giving me something I needed. Deep down, I just knew I wanted to accept because I didn't want to be rude and turn someone down when they were just trying to be kind and helpful. He clearly knew I had just ridden across the Basin where there's no water. This was his home and I didn't want him to think of cyclists as rude people, so I let him fill one of my bottles. After I thanked him for his kindness, I headed up the last climb to Rawlins.

After a nice descent, I found some fast food for lunch in town. I was so grateful to have choices of things to eat and not just eat off my bike. As I finished up, I headed to the gas station to get snacks and a birthday treat. I called Joey, ate some cake and sang him "Happy Birthday." Celebrating over a FaceTime call meant so much to me, even if it was only for five minutes.

Heading out of Rawlins, I thought I was making good time on the road section and would make it to Brush in no time, but, of course, things didn't go as I would have liked. The winds turned, and I had a crosswind almost all afternoon, making the road section slow and extra hard. I was both mentally and physically exhausted from pedaling into the wind and having it push me all over the shoulder most of the afternoon. I met a hiker who was section hiking the Continental Divide, and it was nice to chat and take a little break from the wind. I don't think we crossed paths with the hiking trail often, so it was cool to hear about her experience.

I made it a little further down the road, when I started to realize it might be hard to make it to Brush for the night. I stood on the side of the road crying, just trying to understand why this was so hard for me. When I would call home or talk to another cyclist, they would say, "Just keep going—you're doing great," but I didn't feel like I was doing great. I was tired and crying all the time.

Everything about the day was hard, and missing Joey's birthday had me more emotional than normal. I couldn't even say Brush Mountain without crying. I hadn't even been there, but the thought of missing something I had dreamed of for months and Joey's birthday just left me in tears.

I kept pedaling down the road, trying to hold it together, hoping this moment would pass, still trying to get to Brush Mountain for the night. When it was about midnight, and I still had at least three hours of riding to go, I knew I couldn't make it so I decided that I was going to camp for the night. I was bummed, but I didn't have three or four more hours in me, and the thought of arriving at a lodge at 3 in the morning seemed unreasonable anyway. I found a place to camp, but I felt so deflated after missing Joey's birthday and missing a stay at Brush Mountain Lodge that I cried again as I fell asleep.

June 23: Informal camping before Rawlins, WY, to informal camping (before Brush Mountain), WY

Route Mileage: 1136.44 – 1238.85

Distance: 102.41 miles

Elevation Gain: 5,554 feet

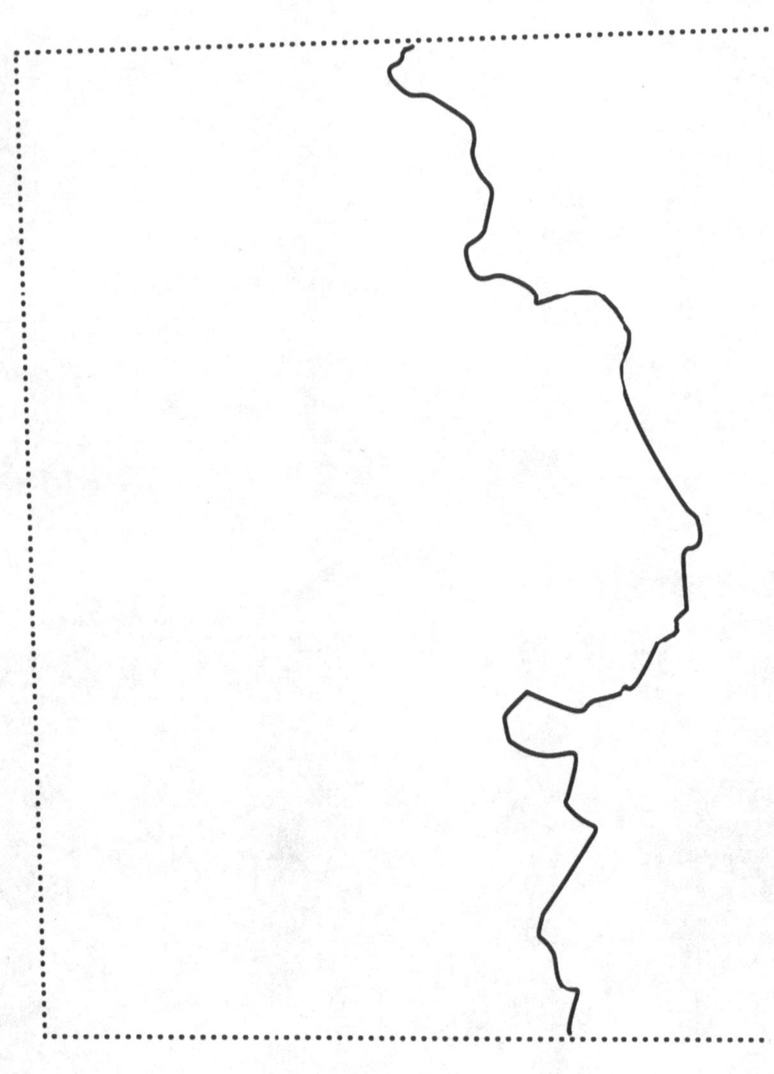

Colorado

Experience the Moment, Not the Place

Day 14 Eager for a fresh day and knowing I would make it to Brush Mountain Lodge, I decided to wake up early. I started down the road as the sun rose. It was a beautiful morning with a blue sky and picture-perfect clouds as I descended from my camp spot to the Colorado border. I was looking forward to crossing the state lines, but Colorado didn't even have a "Welcome to Colorado" sign, which made me laugh. At least Wyoming had a "Leaving Wyoming" sign, so I knew I was moving into my next state.

Just as I passed over the border, I started climbing. I was excited about getting to Brush Mountain Lodge, so it felt like the time flew by, even though it took more than two hours. I was also very nervous about how I would interact with people at Brush. How would I know where to go or who to talk to? From what I had heard, it's different from an average lodge because it is typically only used by touring cyclists and is known for its excellent hospitality on the Divide. I knew this situation would be challenging for me, but this was why I was doing the race: To put myself in situations that shouldn't be scary but are for me.

I arrived at the lodge and noticed there was a picnic table and bike stands so I went over, set some gear down and parked the bike. I was greeted by the owner with the biggest hug, and I had tears in my eyes. She was welcoming and I started to relax. I sat down on the deck and she brought me some hot coffee and the best blueberry pancakes. I was thrilled I had arrived in time for breakfast and coffee because I'm such a breakfast person. I hoped to clean up while at Brush since I couldn't stay the night, and before I could ask, they were showing me inside so I could take a nice, long, hot shower. I washed my clothes and hung them to dry and sat on the deck, watching the hummingbirds and enjoying the quiet.

I still felt disappointed that I wasn't having the whole Brush Mountain Lodge experience that I had dreamed of. As I sat relaxing and waiting for my clothes to dry, I talked with the staff. They told me that they had been watching my dot the night before. Since I had still been moving when they went to bed, they had devised a plan of what to feed me and where I could sleep when I got there. Someone had even set an alarm to wake up around 1:30 a.m. to see where I was. I sat there, shocked by what I was hearing, and there was no way to express how much it meant to find out that people would do this for someone they don't even know. I thanked them all for coming up with such a kind plan and told them I was too nervous to arrive at 3 a.m.—that is one of the reasons I had stopped—but it's fantastic to know that if I had shown up in the middle of the night, they would have been ready for me. It turns out the rumors were true!

I had planned on picking up a new spare derailleur hanger at Orange Peel Bicycle Service in Steamboat, Colorado, but I realized I wasn't going to make it there before they closed. I called Orange Peel using the phone at Brush and asked if they could leave it outside. I paid over the phone, and the staffer said he would set it out at the end of the day, which would work perfectly.

I spent far too much time in the vortex of Brush Mountain Lodge because it was so fun to hang out, have some down time to enjoy my coffee, and spend an afternoon getting ready for the second half of my ride. As I prepared to leave, we had the most Minnesotan goodbye that it took me another hour to get out of there. Before I could go, they needed to get me a PB&J sandwich for lunch, and then, since I didn't get some of her famous wood-fired pizza, the owner made me some peanut butter-bacon sandwiches, too. They were all too amazing. I couldn't be more grateful for the wonderful service and I thought, *You can have the whole Brush Mountain Lodge experience no matter when you arrive.*

When it was really time for me to go, it began to rain, but I had to keep moving. They all thought it was great that I was leaving despite the rain because most people would have turned back around, but I had miles to ride and goals I wanted to achieve. I made it about another 10 minutes up the road when one of the batteries in my shifter stopped working. I carried lots of extra batteries, so it wasn't a big deal, but I struggled to get it working because, for some reason, my shifter didn't like my new battery. Trying not to waste anymore time as I had a lot cycling ahead of me, I put the "dead" one back in, and it worked fine—very odd.

The climb out of Brush was nice and easy until it wasn't. There were a lot of hike-a-bike sections and then a very rocky descent into Steamboat. I slowly made my way down the descent, being careful, but the time was just ticking by so fast and I was moving so slowly. I finally reached Steamboat around midnight; I couldn't believe how long it took me to get there. I headed over to Orange Peel, but they had forgotten to leave the derailleur out. Bummed, I decided I was just going to leave town without it because I didn't want to wait until they opened the next morning. I figured I could look for a new derailleur in Salida, Colorado.

Since it was midnight, I thought about getting a hotel, but I had been warned that the hotels in Steamboat were costly and I shouldn't plan on staying there. I was exhausted, so I searched and searched and only found one room available for the night, which cost more than $300, exactly what I had been warned about. I tried to decide if I should get the room. I debated, back and forth, but I just couldn't do it because $300 for maybe four hours of sleep just didn't seem worth it.

I didn't think there would be any camping options nearby since I was in town, but I looked over the map anyway, and I was right, there was nothing. I just hoped I had enough energy for a couple of hours of riding to find somewhere to camp.

As I headed through town, I just happened to find the perfect place to sleep. There was a baseball field on the side of the road with dugout-style bench seating. Three walls and a top—perfect! It reminded me of our Florida trip when we stayed on a court outside a playground in Key West. I thought this could work: a bench to sleep on that faced toward the field so no one could see me. I laid down on the bench with only my sleeping bag, leaving my helmet on and using it as a pillow. I was so tired I didn't change any of my clothes or even remove my glasses. This was when it became apparent that I would just be exhausted all the time.

June 24: Informal camping, WY, to informal camping in Steamboat Springs, CO

Route Mileage: 1238.85 – 1323.33

Distance: 84.48 miles

Elevation Gain: 8,068 feet

Plan Ahead

Day 15 The baseball dugout was the perfect place to sleep. I woke up dry despite the sprinkling rain the night before, and because I was right in town, there was no snoozing again, as I wanted to make sure no one stumbled upon me. I headed over to a Safeway to get some food before leaving town. As I sat outside eating my donuts, I had a couple of people stop and talk with me, asking about the race because they were surprised to see a female rider. I thought that was funny, but they weren't wrong, I guess. Only a dozen or so women started with the Grand Depart and I had only met one so far.

Leaving Steamboat, there was a detour on the bike path that I decided not to follow. We see those all the time back home, and it never really means anything. When I got about half a mile down the trail though, I realized I *did* need to follow the detour because the trail just ended. As I turned around, I saw two bear cubs playing on the path. I kept my distance, but they were adorable, wrestling around. It reminded me of watching my two kids play when they were little, and it made me so happy. The cubs ran back into the woods quickly when they heard me and I waited a few minutes before proceeding in case their mama was nearby. I kept in mind that best practice is you want to avoid coming between a mom and her cubs.

The morning weather was great with cooler temps and the sun was shining. Making my way out of Steamboat, I hoped to make it to Kremmling, Colorado, for a hotel. It was a nice, paved road, like most roads that left the larger towns, and made for some easy riding. As I was pedaling along, a local cyclist rolled up next to me. We chatted a bit about the race and the wildfires. It was nice to have a little company, even if it was only for 10 minutes.

Even though the riding was easy, I was having another slow-moving morning. I was tired and already eating candy before 9 a.m., so I decided to take a nap. When I woke up, I felt groggy and even more tired. Trying to find a way to wake myself up a little, I decided to change my chain on the side of the road because I was halfway through my trip. I was carrying a spare chain because I didn't know what bike shop supplies would be available since the pandemic had caused supply issues earlier in the year. I thought maybe doing a little work on my bike would help wake me up.

I didn't think through my decision because I got about halfway through the process and then started trying to remember what to do next. Everything seemed harder than it needed to be because I was tired. I finally figured it out and I thought if something had happened and I couldn't get the new chain on the bike or the old chain back on the bike, I was nowhere near a bike shop, and that was poor planning on my part. I wouldn't have been able to bike, and that could have been the end of the ride for me. While I figured it all out, I made a mental note to plan to do repairs near bike shops and not when I was tired and trying to avoid riding my bike.

I started to wake up a little more and the late morning brought a detour around the wildfires in the area. It was nice, because I got to go into the bonus town of Yampa, Colorado, which was a cute town right off the Divide route. I headed over to the local coffee shop for pastries and a hot latte and just happened to pull in right before a huge rainstorm. As I waited for the rain to pass, sipping my coffee, I laid my head down and snoozed a little on the table. When I woke up, I laughed and thought, *I could sleep anywhere.*

The rain stopped so I continued down the road into the afternoon when I could hear helicopters flying overhead, which must have been carrying water for the wildfires. I couldn't believe how close the wildfires were to the route and I was thankful we were able to find a safe way around them.

I slowly kept moving down the road when I came upon a big stream. I wasn't sure how deep it was. Too scared to ride through it, I decided to carry everything across. I hate having wet feet, so I pulled my socks and shoes off and carried everything across in a couple of trips. I was a little annoyed but it felt nice to take my shoes off for a little bit and my feet got a nice cleaning in the freezing cold water.

As I approached the top of the climb in the evening, it started raining. I was planning to get a room in Kremmling, which was a couple of miles off the route. But with poor reception, my phone kept losing its connection. I should have called a hotel earlier in the day but I wasn't confident enough I would make it in time. I kept checking for reception and finally was able to get a call through to a couple of hotels, but they didn't have any rooms. Disappointed, I rode on and thought, *On the bright side, I will at least get close to my 100-mile-per-day goal.* It was after 11 p.m. when it seemed like the rain had stopped, so I set up camp for the night, quickly laying out my sleeping gear and falling right to sleep.

June 25: Informal camping in Steamboat Springs, CO, to informal camping outside Kremmling, CO

Route Mileage: 1323.33 – 1420.20

Distance: 97.51 miles

Elevation Gain: 10,906 feet

Luxuries can be Nice

Day 16 When I woke up, I discovered I had set up camp in a field of cow poop. Great start to my day. I guess I was so tired that I hadn't even noticed it the night before. I was happy I had used my ground cloth and was careful to pack it up in a way that it didn't touch anything else but I still couldn't believe I didn't notice it when I set up camp. I finished packing my bike and headed back down the road.

I was really looking forward to the day because I knew I would make it to Silverthorne, Colorado, and get some Chipotle and Starbucks. I was craving some familiar food. Despite being in these amazing places, getting to a town large enough to have both within walking distance of each other and right on the route felt magical. I remember when I was at that Starbucks in Silverthorne a couple of years earlier, there was a cyclist who was touring the Divide route. Aaron told me how the route goes through town, and I shrugged it off, not really understanding or caring. But now I cared, and I was so excited to get to this familiar place.

The morning brought good riding with a short climb, some descending, and then easy riding into Silverthorne on a bike path, following the river that runs through town. As I approached the strip mall, I was so happy that I had tears in my eyes. I was excited to get food, a big cup of coffee and take a little break. The line at Chipotle was very long, so I went over to Which Wich—which was equally good. The friendly staff greeted me and asked me what I was doing. I told them I was riding my bike across the country. Surprised by my answer, the guy made me a kid's chocolate milk while I waited for my food. He said, "You need the extra calories." I don't normally drink chocolate milk, but it really hit the spot.

I packed up my sandwich and walked over to Starbucks. It was starting to get windy, and the sky slowly changed from blue to gray. It looked like a rainstorm might be rolling in, so I sat inside and started charging my devices. Starbucks took forever to make my order, which gave me time to eat and plan for the rest of the day. But I didn't get to enjoy the drink very long because I needed to get moving before that storm hit Silverthorne. It wasn't raining when I walked outside, but I could see the storm moving slowly toward me, so I rode quickly, trying to make it to Breckenridge, Colorado, without getting wet.

The bike path between the towns was great and a good change of pace, with people out walking and cycling and enjoying the beautiful mountain towns. Just as I got into Breckenridge, I remembered that there is a Starbucks there, too. I was pumped that I could get one more hot coffee before the evening climb.

Breckenridge was so busy. Travel was back on; it was as if COVID-19 had never happened. We were still wearing masks at home, but there was no mask-wearing here. Riding into town, the sidewalks were packed with people, Minnesota State Fair-packed. I parked my bike outside the Starbucks and headed in for coffee when it started pouring. Once the rain started, everyone ducked into buildings. It reminded me again of the Minnesota State Fair, and I felt at home. I got my coffee and sat outside in the rain under an umbrella, watching the weather app. It looked like the rain was only going to last for about an hour, so I waited for it to die down a little since I knew I had a big climb out of Breckenridge. As I stood enjoying my hot white chocolate mocha and the pitter-patter of rain on the umbrella, Aaron's cousins, who live in the area, stopped by to give me hugs. It was nice chatting with them a bit before heading back out for the evening.

I left Breckenridge with the sky still dark gray. I was just hoping the rain would hold off as I started up the climb over Boreas Pass. It was the only climb I had seen before the ride, and I was looking forward to it. I was thinking about how when we had been out in Colorado a couple of years before with friends, Aaron drove us to the top of Boreas Pass because he was so excited to show us part of the Tour Divide route. I remember seeing a cyclist biking up and thinking: *How is he doing that? I would never be able to do that.* Now, just a couple of years later, I was doing it.

As I climbed in my biggest gear, just focusing on riding, a car pulled around me, and two women hopped out with cowbells, cheering. I felt so touched that they had been watching my dot and came out to cheer me on. I started tearing up, just trying to hold it together. It was such good energy. I kept climbing and was slowly losing my daylight, but I didn't care. I just smiled, knowing I was going to make it. Before I knew it, I was on top. It was dark and had started to rain again, so I didn't get to see the view, but I cried happy tears. I was so proud of myself at that moment. Despite a gradual grade for over 10 miles, I'd ridden all the way up without walking. It wasn't even as hard as I had thought it would be. I thought to myself, *Sometimes the climbs don't seem worth the effort, but when I get to the top, no matter how hard, it is always worth it because I accomplish something that seemed impossible only weeks ago.*

I pulled myself together and bundled up for the descent. I put on my puffy jacket under my raincoat, and I wore my winter mittens for the first time. With the cold rain, the descent was a lot less fun than the climb. I could hardly see with the rain hitting my glasses.

The road seemed in terrible shape, but I didn't know if it was that bad or if I was just not seeing well because my glasses kept fogging up. I was shivering, and my hands hurt from braking so hard. I took my time, trying not to crash. I couldn't wait to be done. I felt like I spent more time descending than climbing, which was so frustrating.

When I finally made it to the bottom, or what I thought was the bottom, I checked my data sheet and saw there was camping outside the community building in Como, Colorado. I just needed to make it there and I would stay the night. Trying to warm up as the road slowly flattened out, I couldn't wait to get out of my wet clothes.

I arrived in town just after 11 p.m., but it was so small it was hardly a town. I finally saw a building that I thought was the community center and school. I just crossed my fingers and hoped that no one would yell at me if they found me there in the morning. I tucked in close to the building, as far away from the tall, wet grass as possible. I smiled, remembering the great day I had had, with coffee, food and the realization of just how far I'd come in my riding, with 1,000 miles to go.

June 26: Informal camping outside Kremmling, CO, to informal camping in Como, CO

Route Mileage: 1420.20 – 1504.29

Distance: 83.45 miles

Elevation Gain: 9,098 feet

Sometimes a Break is Needed

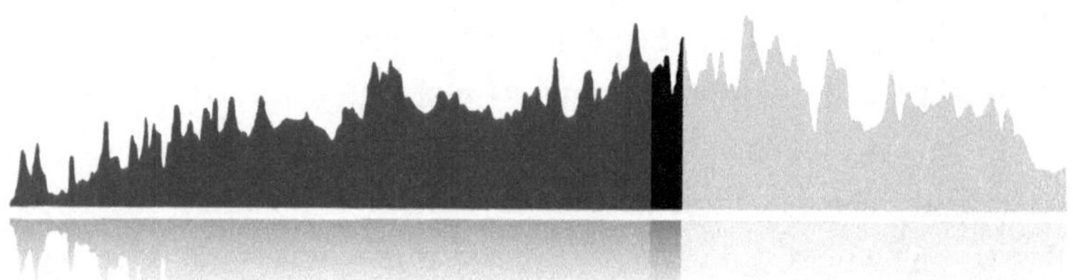

Day 17 I packed up my bike, hoping my overnight stop in Como would give the roads time to dry. I set out down the road, hoping it wouldn't be too muddy and enjoying the quiet. I passed ranches full of horses, and I was excited to show Molly all the pictures when we talked. I told her I would try to take a picture of every horse I saw during the ride because they all reminded me of her!

I arrived in Hartsel, Colorado, and found a restaurant for breakfast. I headed right inside to start charging my devices before returning outside, where I laid out my gear to dry. I was finally figuring out this multitasking business.

After missing Joey's birthday and now Molly's, I knew this was going to be a tough day mentally. I realize that may sound silly, but birthdays are important to me and just as important to Molly, and it was hard not to be there with her. I know Joey was sad that I missed his birthday, but I knew Molly was sadder not to have her mom and best friend with her, which made it hard for me.

I headed back inside to eat and keep charging my devices before calling the birthday girl! As I sat at the table planning my day,

I saw that I was headed for Salida, Colorado, another great town for bike service and food supplies. Salida is our family's favorite spot to stop in Colorado and it seemed fitting to arrive there on such a special day. I packed up my things and headed back outside to call Molly, hoping I could have an uplifting conversation and not focus on how sad I was. We had a nice chat and managed to make it through without any tears, which was a huge win. I felt so good after talking to her that I knew it was going to be a great day on my bike.

As I rode out of Hartsel, the landscape was beautiful, with an open range and mountains as the backdrop. It was relatively flat with rolling roads, and I really could not complain about a flat-ish stretch at this point. I was taking my time and enjoying the beautiful day because the weather was perfect, the riding was manageable and everything seemed good. As I approached the short, steep climb before descending into Salida, I was getting excited to be so close to town. I got to the top just as it started raining, which seemed to happen to me every day. Descending into Salida, I got soaked and covered in mud.

I turned off the route to head into town so I could stop by Absolute Bikes to see if they had the derailleur hanger I was still looking for. They did not and sent me to SubCulture Cyclery. The mechanic there had one on hand, so I finally got a replacement derailleur. I was very hopeful I would not need it, but then, that is what I said about the first one. He suggested I wash my bike because the Salida mud can be bad for it and then asked if I needed to shower because they had one, which made me laugh. I had no idea what he was talking about with the Salida mud, but I assumed he was right because he lived there. I took him up on the bike wash and rinsed the bike, but I passed on the shower.

I headed over to the Safeway for food, snacks and birthday cake of some sort just as it started raining again. I quickly went inside and called Molly to eat cake and celebrate with her before she went to bed. As we started to talk, I began to cry. I was upset and jealous about not being home to celebrate with everyone. Now it was raining, which meant that although it wasn't even 7 p.m., it felt darker and later than it was. I was wet and tired, and when I looked at my miles for the day, I had only ridden 76 and thought, *I am never going to finish this ride*. I asked to talk to Aaron, because I needed a minute. I couldn't help but feel sad when I talked to Molly.

I told Aaron that I was thinking about stopping for the day but if I stopped now, there would be more miles to make up the next eight days, and I didn't have the time, but I also didn't want to ride anymore. I was an emotional mess. I weighed my options: ride, or rest and sleep. While part of me wanted to keep going, part of me said, *You need a break*. I decided I would look for a hotel. I got lucky —the Salida Hostel had a last-minute cancellation. I could have the room if I got there by 8 p.m. I took that as a sign that I needed to stop for the day. I told Molly I would call her back after I got checked into the hostel. I quickly headed over to the Salida Hostel, which was right off the route, another great reason that this was the right choice as I wouldn't have to backtrack in the morning—perfect!

The hostel was cute with walls covered in murals and maps, matching the décor of this mountain town. I asked the desk clerk if I could drag my bike upstairs, and she said it was no problem. Even though I felt bad about doing that in this pretty place, I needed my bike. I took a shower and started my laundry before heading back to the Safeway for a couple more items. I had been in such a hurry to check in, I had forgotten to get sunscreen and thought I should grab more food. I got back to my room and called Molly back to chat, eat cake and sing "Happy Birthday" with everyone over FaceTime, again. It was so nice to hear all about her day, and I was happy that I had decided to stay. I needed a break and to have that moment with Molly. I laid out my gear to dry overnight and finally headed to bed just after 10 p.m. I was a little down about my mileage but happy to have a bed to sleep in and some FaceTime with the family.

June 27: Informal camping in Como, CO, to Salida, CO

Route Mileage: 1504.29 – 1580.72

Distance: 76.43 miles

Elevation Gain: 5,154 feet

Sleep can be Golden

Day 18 Waking after a good night's sleep felt so nice. I felt refreshed and ready for another full day of biking. I let myself sleep in until almost 6 a.m. and sat down to enjoy hot coffee and muffins in the hostel. With a little extra time to prepare myself for the last leg of the trip, I was feeling ready to start the day with a big climb. Marshall Pass is well known for being a very long climb—26.2 miles from Salida, which is a marathon of climbing. For the most part, I thought the grade looked rideable, but that's still a long way to ride up.

As I headed outside, the weather was great and I was really looking forward to another day on the Divide. I started up the climb, and the riding was perfect. I knew it would take a while to climb the entire pass, but I was ready to be patient with myself. I knew it would be hard but I wanted to focus on trying to enjoy the beauty of Colorado and not the hours of climbing. Partway up the pass, I looked over the edge to see a beautiful crystal-clear lake where I saw tons of people camping.

I kept steadily climbing up the pass while taking some breaks to walk and push my bike, too. A touring cyclist passed me, which embarrassed me because I should have been riding my bike, not pushing it, but my legs needed a break and it felt nice to walk for a bit. It seemed like it took forever but when I finally reached the top of the pass at over 10,800 feet where it levels out and intersects with the Colorado Trail, it was so beautiful! I could see all the way down to the town I had just come from. It was a remarkable feeling knowing I had just made it to the top.

I snapped some photos before it started to rain a little, but nothing like the other days. At this point in the ride, I just assumed that if I was going down, I was getting rained on. It had happened every day in Colorado so far. The road down was incredible— smooth, fast gravel. I couldn't believe how quickly I made it to the bottom and got to Tomichi Creek Trading Post by lunch time.

I went inside and found some cyclists who invited me to sit down with them. One of the riders was another Minnesotan touring the route and the other was a rider who told us all about the many issues he had encountered during the ride thus far. Most recently, he had made a fire the night before to dry his clothes, and the clothes caught on fire, leaving everything with holes in it. He told us about how he had six flats the first day, had to replace his bike (yes, the entire bike) and the new bike's seat stay took some damage to the carbon frame, so it was taped back together. I felt lucky that the only bike issue I had had so far was my fault, and I fixed it rather quickly the next day. I hadn't had any flats, mechanical issues, bag or zipper failures, and all my gear was working as planned. I was carrying all my repair gear but hadn't needed it yet, and, hopefully, I wouldn't need to use it at all.

It was nice to share the lunch table with other cyclists and not just talk to myself or look at my maps. The brief conversation lifted my mood. I hadn't realized how lonely I was feeling at times, until I had someone to talk to. The two guys were just finishing lunch when I sat down, but I ate quickly so I could leave with them and ride with them for even just 15 minutes. I knew I could never keep up, but it was an excellent way to get me moving quickly after lunch. The riding the rest of the afternoon was nice, with smooth gravel and no major climbs into the evening, which made for a quick end to my day.

Watching the sunset over the valley fill the sky with pink and purple hues was amazing and the perfect cap to my day. I realized a good night's sleep had given me what I needed to push through a long day and hit my 100-plus miles-per-day goal. I started to think, *Maybe I can finish this*.

June 28: Salida, CO, to informal camping, CO
Route Mileage: 1580.72 – 1691.34
Distance: 110.62 miles
Elevation Gain: 7,648 feet

Adjust Your Expectations

Day 19 My day started with climbing, which wasn't my favorite way to start, but it had become a trend: start a climb at night, get tired, go to sleep, start the next morning on a climb.

Although the riding was easy and uneventful, I was moving slowly. I thought having such a great day the day before would carry over, but I just didn't have enough energy to move any quicker. As the morning pressed on, the route turned into some single-track trail for a few miles. I was not in the mood for any single track. I really hadn't ridden much single track before this ride and I was struggling just to stay on the trail. I was upset one second and laughing the next because I was so terrible at it. Even though this wasn't even a technical single-track trail, it wasn't my thing. It took me far too long to get through that section, and I was beating myself up. When the single track finally ended and I was back on gravel roads, I couldn't have been happier.

As I turned the corner to start the last miles into Del Norte, Colorado, I saw a man standing by his car with a cooler. I rode over to him and he introduced himself as Steve. The name sounded so familiar, and then he said, "I met Aaron on the Tour Divide." I was confused for a moment, not really understanding what he meant. Then it came to me. I said, "Oh! Are you Single Speed Steve?" and we had a good laugh. Steve rode the Divide the year Aaron did, on a single-speed bike (one gear) for 2,700 miles, which is so incredible. I was hardly doing it with all my gears; I couldn't imagine having only one. I thanked him for being out to support riders as I headed to town for lunch.

I stopped at the gas station as I entered town and it had a Subway, so I decided I would get a sandwich instead of eating at a sit-down restaurant to cut down on my stop time. While eating my sandwich, I had a lot to think about. I had been contemplating for days what I should do because the idea of finishing the route was feeling a bit out of reach. The day before had gone so well and I had felt so confident. Now, I was moving slowly and not feeling that way at all. With only six days left of riding, I was worried. For days, all I had needed to do was ride 5 more miles a day, which could be over an hour of riding at this point. But every day I didn't ride those 5 extra miles, they would get added to the next day's ride. I started to think I probably wouldn't finish, because most days I wasn't even riding my 100-miles-per-day goal, so how could I ride the 105 or 110 miles a day I needed to finish in my time off? It no longer seemed possible to complete the miles I had left on my days off.

I thought: *What if I had one more day? Could I finish the route if I had one more day to ride?*

I did some math and thought if I had more time, I could do it. I decided that I needed to ask for more days off from work so I could finish the entire route. I also knew, deep down inside, that I would not be happy if I didn't finish the route. I had said so many times: *I'm just going to ride for 25 days. It doesn't matter if I don't finish.* But I knew it did matter. That was just a cover story, so I wouldn't be disappointed in myself if I didn't make it.

While I sat there, I stared at my phone. I was typing and retyping the message, deleting, changing and deciding if I could hit send. I thought my boss would say yes to a couple more days off work but I felt anxious and embarrassed that I needed more time. Finally, I hit send. And I waited for those three little typing dots. My stomach hurt, and it felt like it was taking forever, but it was only one minute. He responded, "Yeah ... Just keep having fun." I don't know why I was so nervous, because I knew it wouldn't be a big deal.

While I told myself leading up to the trip that 25 days was my max, it was a relief to know I had the time to complete what I had started. I appreciated the support from my boss and everything he and our team did so I could make this happen. I knew I could finish and I was happy that I got to keep riding even if that wasn't what I originally planned.

I loaded the bike with food and started out of Del Norte with so much joy. The afternoon started with a climb. I was starting to realize that when I climbed in the afternoons, it meant I made especially slow progress. I saw a lot more northbound cyclists, and it was fun to chat a little with people as they would come by. They would tell me about what was to come, which wasn't always what I wanted to hear, things like "Oooh, it's kinda rocky and steep." I kept slowly climbing up Indiana Pass until I was too tired to continue and found a camp spot for the night. It had been an emotional day, realizing how important it was to me to finish this route, no matter how long it took.

June 29: Informal camping, CO, to informal camping (north of Platoro) on Indiana Pass (through Del Norte mid-day), CO

Route Mileage: 1691.34 –1755.44

Distance: 64.10 miles

Elevation Gain: 6,214 feet

Every Experience has a Purpose

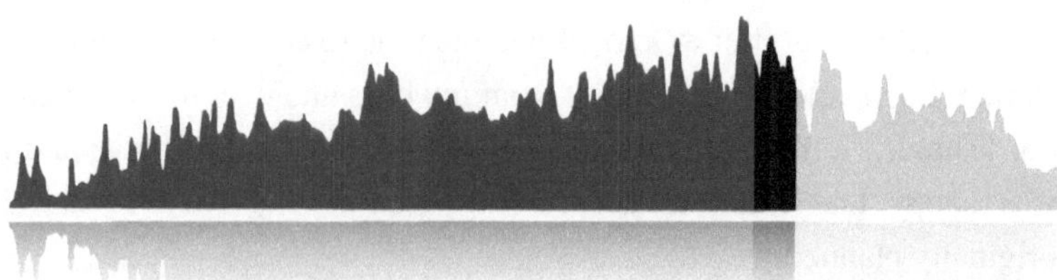

Day 20 My alarm went off, and I snoozed it a couple of times before I finally got out of my bivy at 5:15 a.m. knowing I needed to finish Indiana Pass. I was not excited about the early morning, but I had just gotten more time to finish the route so I couldn't jeopardize finishing by sleeping in.

The climb was challenging first thing in the morning. I was tired but I needed to keep moving, even if it was slow, just to make progress up the pass. I topped the high point of the pass and after some short, little climbs before Platoro, Colorado, I was getting hungry and really looking forward to breakfast. In Platoro, I found a cute little restaurant with a store attached, so while I waited for my food, I picked up some more snacks for the day. They had homemade fudge, and I have a soft spot for fudge, so I bought enough for the whole day. I went outside to hang up some wet gear before heading back to my table to eat. It wasn't the best breakfast I have ever had, but food is food when you're hungry and need to eat.

The afternoon was lovely with no significant climbs and so much time to think. While I had been out here for 20 days at this point, I had thought about everything from random yard projects I would tackle when I got home to different things I should try for dinner. I would talk to my dad as if he could hear me, and I thought a lot about home life, hoping everyone was having a great time. I couldn't help but smile as I knew I was getting close to being done and would see everyone soon.

I was listening to my book and enjoying the moment when a rider I had seen several times came by and asked, "Why are you always wearing headphones?" Confused about why it mattered, I said "I enjoy listening to music and audiobooks." But for some reason, it really bothered me that he had even asked.

I couldn't stop thinking about his comment. I thought: *Why should I not listen to music, podcasts or audiobooks? Should I just be here only in the sounds of nature? Some people like to sit on a beach and enjoy a great book; we don't think twice about that. I enjoy riding my bike and listening to novels. Beaches are not my thing, but biking all day is.* It was hard to not focus on what he had said when I had so much time to think. I knew I didn't need to worry about what anyone else thought, but I did and it's hard not to sometimes.

I returned to my audio book and tried to enjoy the rest of the afternoon, simply riding my bike, eating food and taking in the beauty of Colorado. I passed a sign that meant I was leaving Colorado and going into New Mexico, and I had never been so excited to be in a new state. There was so much joy in knowing I was going into my last state.

Feeling energized, I switched to some music and listened to my trip theme song, "Get Back Up Again." As the days passed, I realized how much it helped to lift my mood. It may seem like a silly song, but its message of resilience and perseverance to keep going even when there are setbacks, to find the strength and determination to come back, day after day, and to keep moving forward even when it is hard really resonated with me on my ride. It had been a hard day with my thoughts focused on someone else's negative ideas. I needed to listen to this song.

I kept pedaling late into the night, worrying about my miles but trying not to. I checked the map, the elevation and then looked at the time, hoping I could somehow get more miles in before it got too late, but I didn't move any faster and the time just kept ticking away. It was 1 a.m. and I was only at 85 miles. While I was happy to be in my final state, New Mexico, I was worried about not getting in 100 miles again. I headed to bed, realizing that while anyone can have an opinion, I need to only care about what works for me.

June 30: Informal camping, CO, to informal camping, NM
Route Mileage: 1755.44 – 1841.14
Distance: 85.70 miles
Elevation Gain: 10,361 feet

BAKERS TANK
MILE POST 102.16

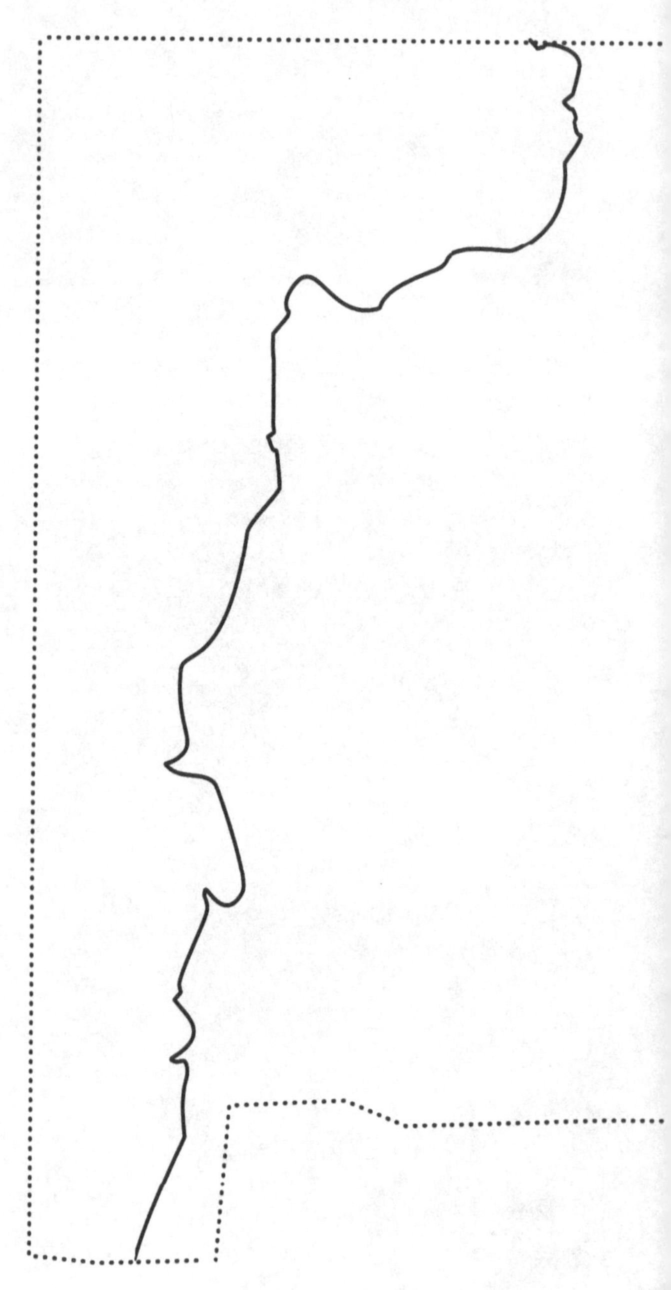

New Mexico

Appreciate the Small Things

Day 21 I woke up and noticed my phone battery percentage was low. After 20 days, I was still having issues keeping my electronics charged. It wasn't like things were dead, but I would forget to put my phone in airplane mode or leave my AirPods plugged in all night, which drained my portable charger. Those were silly mistakes to still be making this far into my trip. With only a few days left, I was not sure I would get another hotel so I was searching for a new iPhone charging cord with a USB on one end instead of the USB-C I had brought. I couldn't charge my phone off the bike or my backup portable charger until I could find a new cable. I really should have thought through my charging situation better before I left home. But for now, I needed to find a new cable.

I was hoping for a higher mileage day since the day before I only did 85 miles. After I rode for a bit and warmed up, I stopped for breakfast, as I did most days, and looked over my maps. I was starting to realize that the more elevation I had in a day reduced the miles I could complete, and with back-to-back, high elevation-gain days, I needed to not focus on the miles and just ride my bike. But, easier said than done.

With lots of climbing in the morning, it was slow going, but I was trying to be patient as I knew the afternoon would level out. Just after lunch I got to another milestone: Silva's Store. Best known from the "Ride the Divide" film, it's a little snack shop in the middle of a tiny community, right on the route. After a quick stop for some treats, I kept on my way to Abiquiu, New Mexico, still in search of an iPhone cable.

I rode through El Rito, New Mexico, where I stopped at a shop to see if they had a charging cable in case I didn't make it to Abiquiu in time. By now, I knew I couldn't get anywhere in the time I thought I could and was always thinking about the worst-case scenario. There was a group of men in the store who asked me all about the race, and I was so appreciative that they seemed to care. One man said, "If you do a shot, I will buy you anything in the store." I kindly turned him down, but he insisted on paying for my things. With no phone cords, I grabbed some food and got on my way.

I was focused on getting that cable so I could charge my phone and the miles flew by. I wanted my audiobooks; it was all I could think about—a great distraction. It was a quick 15 miles to Abiquiu with all paved roads and a nice shoulder for riding. When I got to town, I went straight to the Family Dollar to find a phone cord. All I could find was a 6-foot cord, but I didn't even care; I was so happy to be able to charge my phone again. I walked to the restaurant across the street, but it had closed at 7 p.m. and it was now 7:10. I hadn't even thought to check the hours because I was so focused on getting that cable. I guess I should have stopped there first since the Family Dollar was open until 9 p.m. The woman inside the restaurant saw me outside and offered to reopen, which was so kind. She said they had some pastries left over from the day, so I grabbed something for dinner and breakfast the next day. I was grateful for her willingness to open back up when she saw me outside.

Just as I was packing up my bike, another rider rolled up. He told me he knew who I was because he had been watching me on the

Trackleaders page to see when I would catch him, which made me laugh. He got separated from the group he was riding with that day because of a bike issue but was going to try to catch them in the morning. He was also looking for dinner, and I suggested he go to the order window of the restaurant. He made me laugh when he told her, "My friend over there said you might have food left," even though we had just met. Somehow on the Divide, it didn't matter when you met, everyone was bonded by this adventure.

I returned to the Family Dollar and asked if I could charge my electronics inside since I couldn't charge at the restaurant. The cashier was helpful and found a place where I could plug everything in, which just happened to be in their seasonal aisle in the middle of the store. I laughed as I plugged in over the swimming accessories.

With some extra juice on the electronics, I packed up the bike with food and went in search of somewhere to camp. The rider from the restaurant and I left town together and we rode up the road, past a neighborhood with barking dogs. I was happy to have someone to ride with because there were so many dogs out. We found a camping spot about 5 miles up the road and I decided on an early night because I knew the climb the next day would be tough. In my bivy, I thought about how remarkable it was that I was still meeting new riders this far into my trip, but I loved it.

July 1: Informal camping, NM, to informal camping just past Abiquiu, NM

Route Mileage: 1841.14 – 1927.18

Distance: 86.04 miles

Elevation Gain: 8,035 feet

We All Need a Good Cry from Time to Time

Day 22 After snoozing my alarm a couple of times and seeing two groups of riders go by, I thought it was time to get moving. I knew I had about 30 miles of climbing ahead of me. The early morning roads were pretty good, and I was feeling good about my morning miles, but as soon as I had that thought, the road started to have substantial rock plates that were difficult for me ride over. I got frustrated trying to ride on them, and to be pushing my bike as other riders passed me felt terrible. It was odd to feel embarrassed because I had made it this far, but I didn't want anyone to know how hard this was for me. I was exhausted every moment of every day. In my head, the other riders were all sleeping in because it wasn't as difficult for them, even if that wasn't actually the case.

As I neared the top, I could see a storm filling the sky. During the first storm of my trip, back in Montana, I was at the bottom of the pass, and I remembered feeling so nervous, not knowing what to do. Now I felt a lot more comfortable. Near the top of the pass, I knew to stay under the tree line, but stay alert for lightning nearby. I found a place to take a break, tucked under some trees and napped for a little bit while the rain passed. There wasn't lightning, just rain, and a little nap felt really nice. When I started riding again, I thought I was at the top, but I wasn't. There were still these three little humps I had to get over, just like at Union Pass, and I was very irritated. I made it over the last section and thought, *Sweet, I will get some downhill*, but instead it just flattened out.

The climb was challenging that morning, there was no descending after hours of climbing, and I was exhausted. I couldn't control my emotions and didn't know what to do with them. Feeling overwhelmed with how challenging everything had been, I called Aaron when I finally got cell reception and, in tears, told him I didn't know if I could keep going. I was emotionally exhausted and physically tired and questioned why I was still riding. I knew I had to keep going, but I felt like everything was out of my control. I just kept crying. I didn't understand why I was so emotional. I hated that I cried so much, yet crying was the only thing that helped. I thought: *How could I get through the rest of today, or even to the end? I still have over 500 miles ahead of me*. But I just had to keep moving, so I pulled myself together the best I could. I told myself, *Just make it to Cuba, New Mexico; no decision can be made when you're this emotional*.

I pulled myself together and continued moving down the trail before hitting a paved road with a steep descent into Cuba. It felt nice to ride the brakes instead of pedaling for just a moment. Just a couple of miles out from Cuba, some dogs started to chase me. One got so close to me I could feel the warmth of his mouth on my leg. I tried not to panic but I was so tired, I couldn't think of what to do. I tried to unclip, but that didn't happen, so I stood up with a hard pedal stroke forward to quickly get away from the dogs. My heart was pounding, but luckily, I didn't get bitten.

I turned a corner and was in Cuba. What a relief! I was ready for this day to be over, to find something to eat and to get a good night's rest. I had a voicemail message from a rider when I got to town; he had a motel room and asked if I wanted it. He planned to shower, charge his devices and continue riding through the night so I could sleep in the room after he left. It sounded like the perfect plan.

I got to the motel and saw on Trackleaders that the other group of guys who were right ahead of me were at the same motel. I had been seeing their dots on Trackleaders for a couple of days now. I was excited to meet them all since I knew one was from Minnesota. First, I went to get some food, and as I was walking back from the gas station, I noticed everyone who was riding had their doors open, bouncing in and out of each other's rooms. I settled in my room, and then I popped my head into the room next door to introduce myself, and everyone responded, "It's Mary!" It caught me off guard, that all these guys I'd been half a day behind for days had all been watching my dot and waiting for me to catch them. I didn't know their names, but having all these people recognize me as a racer was a special moment. I started to feel like maybe I was in the race.

I briefly chatted with the guys before we all headed to bed. They said they were leaving at 4 a.m. the following day to get a good jump on the long road section and invited me to leave with them, which sounded great. I knew the easiest way to make myself get up early was to commit to doing it with others. When I told our plan for the morning to the guy who had offered to share his motel room, he decided that seemed better than riding through the night, so we ended up sharing the room. I slept on the floor again, but I had a place to charge my devices for the final days, a hot shower and a dry place to sleep.

As I lay on the motel floor, thinking how gross the carpet was, I couldn't believe that hours earlier in the day, I had been crying and saying I didn't know if I could keep going, and now I was setting an alarm for 3:30 a.m. I knew I wouldn't stop, but it had felt good to let out a good cry and then move on.

July 2: Informal camping outside Abiquiu, NM, to Cuba, NM

Route Mileage: 1927.18 – 1999.66

Distance: 72.48 miles

Elevation Gain: 9,065 feet

Sometimes, Take a Nap

Day 23 3:30 a.m. is early. It wasn't easy waking up but knowing I had a group to ride with motivated me to get out of bed. I got ready quickly and headed outside to find that about half of us were ready to go at 4 a.m., and some were a little slower. By about 4:10, we decided to leave with whoever was there. It felt like a mini-Grand Depart to the finish. There must have been about 12 of us, including some touring cyclists, so it was really exciting.

I had checked the map the night before and knew that the entire day would be on pavement, which made me both happy and nervous. I knew it would be easier riding, but the pavement and cars still scared me. I rode with the group for a couple of miles at their very fast pace, but it wasn't sustainable for me since I knew I would be out there all day, so I separated from the large group. One of the touring cyclists also slowed down a bit, and we rode together. It was fun to have someone to chat with for a while, and we had some random things in common, like both being twins from the Midwest with a running background.

I needed to make a quick pitstop, and then I was back alone. It was a long, hot day with only one resupply option, which I somehow missed. There was one water spot a little off route, so I gave that a shot, but a man was filling up his truck with water so I couldn't use it. He said the water wasn't really for bottles, anyway, and offered to fill my water bottles from his truck. I said it was okay and thanked him. Another kind person—it never stopped.

Time was moving so slowly. I felt like I was taking breaks every five minutes to eat or go to the bathroom or find any reason not to be riding. Then, I started taking 10-minute naps every couple of hours on the side of the road, and that seemed to help, or at least gave me something to look forward to. I didn't know if I was tired from the heat or a lack of food or maybe I was just bored, but it was a long day. I felt like I was making no progress again. I tried to focus on anything except how much riding sucked at that moment. When I looked at my miles for the day, I realized I was actually doing pretty well, and I magically started feeling better.

Getting close to Grants, New Mexico, I was feeling great, singing and smiling because I knew there were food options for dinner and I had 120 miles for the day at just past 6 p.m. I found a pizza place and got some dinner and a calzone for the next day. I thought I was ordering a personal-size calzone, but it turned out it was a family-size one, so I guessed I would be eating calzones for a while. As I was eating my dinner, I thought about getting a hotel in Grants. But it was just past 7 p.m. when I finished dinner, and I needed to get in a couple more hours of riding if I could.

As I biked down the main street of Grants, chairs lined the road in preparation for the 4th of July parade. It reminded me of when we would visit Aaron's Granny in her small town in southern Minnesota, where they had parades for Turkey Day. The night before, everyone set up chairs to claim their spots. We do the same things in small towns from Minnesota to New Mexico, which made me smile.

As I left Grants, my knee started to hurt a little. It was the first time I had been in physical pain during the ride, and I was a little nervous. I kept pedaling, hoping it just hurt because I was tired from the long day and faster pace on the pavement. After a while, it wasn't feeling any better so I decided to start looking for a place to camp. I was hoping a good night's rest would help my knee work itself out.

After almost 140 miles for the day, which was great for me, I found a campground off the main road. I felt bad getting there so late because one of the campers' dogs started barking at me as I tried to find a place to sleep. I turned off my lights and found a spot away from the dog and he finally settled down. I set my alarms and was happy to get some rest after a long day in the saddle.

July 3: Cuba, NM, to Joe Skeen Campground (BLM), NM
Route Mileage: 1999.66 – 2139.54
Distance: 139.88 miles
Elevation Gain: 4,462 feet

People Come into Your Life for a Reason

Day 24 Leaving the campground at 5 a.m., I hit the pavement for another 20 miles, which was an excellent start to my day. My knee didn't hurt, which is exactly what I had hoped for, and I knew it would be a good day. With a stop in Pie Town, New Mexico, ahead of me, I was excited for a personal-size pie.

I was thinking about when Aaron did the Tour Divide in 2019 and Salsa Cycles handed out stem caps. If you made it to Pie Town, you could show the stem cap to get a free pie. I was disappointed when I found out Salsa was not doing that this year, but I was still looking forward to my personal pie. It wasn't about the free pie, though free is always good. I just thought it was so cool that people carried their stem cap for over 2,000 miles with the reward of a free pie for making it all the way there.

I was aiming to get there by mid-morning because I had heard that they sometimes run out of pie if you get there too late in the day. Since it was the 4th of July and pie is a staple celebratory dessert, I didn't want to take any chances. So, I really needed to focus on riding and nothing else.

As I got into Pie Town, the guys from yesterday were just leaving. I wasn't racing them, but it was nice to know they hadn't gotten too far ahead of me the day before. I started my meal alone at a long table in the outdoor seating area, and a cute, little kitten joined me. He was crawling all over the table and bench and then laid right next to me for a little company.

Then, a group sat down to share the table. We talked about my trip and what I was doing. They were genuinely interested and in awe that anyone could ride their bike this far. One woman was tearing up. I thought to myself, *It's sweet they are impressed with me, because I don't feel that what I am doing is that amazing.* I really doubted myself in moments like this, feeling like I am such a slow rider and not cool enough to deserve their praise. As we continued to talk, she compared me to the people on "Survivor," which is such a compliment since I love that show and I could only wish to be cool enough to be on "Survivor." We finished lunch and they paid for my pie, which brought tears to my eyes. I was learning that what might seem simple to me, just riding my bike, didn't always seem that way to other people. Their kind words meant so much to me and helped me realize how inspiring I could be to others.

After I had eaten my entire pie, I made my way back to the route but I could hardly move. I passed the Toaster House Hostel, just a couple of minutes past the restaurant, and I thought about stopping but decided I had to keep pedaling—I had places to be! Not two minutes later, I turned back. I needed to sleep off some of this food. When I got to the Toaster House, my stomach hurt badly. I hadn't eaten that much food in so long; it was taking a toll. I needed a nap.

I slept for about an hour and I felt much better when I woke up. With a full tummy and good energy from my lunch friends, I put in some big miles that afternoon, hitting a little peanut butter mud but nothing I couldn't handle. There was a little sprinkle of rain in the late afternoon, but I stayed pretty dry.

As it got dark, I started to see lights in the sky in all directions. At first, I thought it was a lightning storm but then remembered that it was the 4th of July. I knew Aaron and the kids were on their way to meet me, and I wondered where they had stopped to watch fireworks. I was sad that we weren't spending the 4th of July together, but I enjoyed looking up to the sky, knowing we were all looking at them together. They may have been watching different fireworks, but at least we were in the same state again.

July 4: Joe Skeen Campground (BLM), NM, to informal camping, NM

Route Mileage: 2139.54 – 2251.09

Distance: 111.55 miles

Elevation Gain: 6,411 feet

Don't Take Time for Granted

Day 25 With an early start to the day, I wanted to do as many miles as possible because this was, originally, supposed to be my last day of riding. I was down, knowing I wasn't going to finish today, but also grateful that I had been given the time to keep going. I had thought about this day for so long. When things were hard, I would say, *One more day.* But day 25 came, and I still had more than 200 miles to go.

While riding that morning, I passed another rider having issues with his tubes holding air. I told him he should flag me down if he needed anything. But then I remembered that I had missed so much while riding. Other riders would ask me if I saw things, and I had no idea what they were talking about. It was as if I wasn't even riding the same roads. Sometimes, I was just in my zone and not noticing anything around me. I told him that if he needed help, he should sit in the middle of the road so I didn't miss him. We had a good laugh, and I kept going.

Midafternoon, I made it to Beaverhead Outfitters and ate lunch in the shade, because it had been a hot morning with no cloud cover. Before the trip, a couple of people had told me that there was a soda pop machine at Beaverhead Outfitters. While there probably wouldn't be any people there, you could use this random soda machine in the middle of nowhere. I had carried change during the entire trip to get a soda there, but when I got there, the soda machine was unplugged. Disappointed, I drank water with my lunch.

I started out from Beaverhead Outfitters and an hour later, a huge rainstorm came in. It was a hard, cold rain that, luckily, didn't last long. But I went from being extremely hot to extremely cold in just a few hours. I was wet for the rest of the evening and was moving very slowly because of it. I couldn't warm up, and strong streams ran over the road. I had to carry my bike several times because I was in the forest with the tree cover shading the road and I couldn't tell how deep the water was. I kept biking and walking through water until I finally started a climb and the streams stopped.

As I made my way up the climb, I warmed up a little, which was nice, but now I needed to eat. I was soaked and nervous about stopping because I didn't want to get cold after I had just warmed up. I finally decided I needed to put on some dry clothes so I could eat. Otherwise, I wouldn't be able to keep going. It was just about 10 p.m., and there was a campground maybe 10 miles down the road that I wanted to get to so I could set myself up for a successful last day. I would have more than 150 miles to ride, but I knew I could do it. I had done a 140-mile day on paved roads a couple of days ago, and there would be quite a bit of paved roads to the finish. I took out my stove and warmed water for ramen noodles. I changed my clothes before packing up the bike and heading to the campground.

As I made my way down the road, I started to feel very drowsy. I looked down at my Wahoo only to realize I had only made it 1 mile. I wanted to keep going to the campground down the road, but I couldn't keep my eyes focused enough to ride. I decided to stop so I didn't get hurt and I pulled just off the road, in the only area I could find. I set out my bivy, not blowing up my sleeping pad up for the 10th night in row, because I didn't want to spend any extra time on it. I was a little bummed I hadn't made it as far as I wanted and it was pretty early for me, but I couldn't keep my eyes open and I fell right to sleep.

July 5: Informal camping, NM, to informal camping before Lake Roberts, NM

Route Mileage: 2251.09 – 2326.51

Distance: 75.42 miles

Elevation Gain: 9,544 feet

Happiness is a Choice

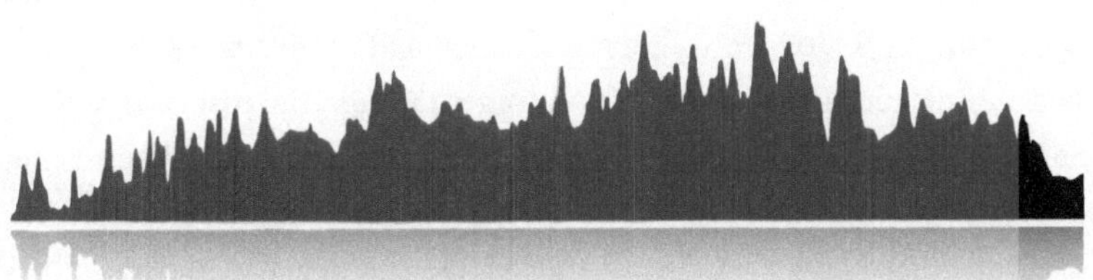

Day 26 I got out of my bivy and packed up my bike and for the first time, I couldn't remember what direction I had come from the night before. As a general rule, at night you always point your bike in the direction you are going, but when I woke up and picked up my bike, I couldn't remember which way it had been facing. It was still dark and early, just before 4 a.m., and I was tired. After about 10 minutes, I figured out the right direction to start going, even though I wasn't fully awake.

It was a bittersweet day, knowing that I needed to bike to Antelope Wells today, no matter if I finished at 11 p.m. or 3 a.m., and knowing that today would be my last day of riding. I still had 170 miles left so it seemed unbelievable to think I was planning on finishing, but I'd done a big day before and knew I could do it again. I just kept telling myself, *You can do this*.

I got to the campground, the one I had hoped to get to the night before, and made breakfast, dried my clothes, and filled up my water because this was my last stop until Silver City, New Mexico. The roads into Silver City were paved, which was nice, but the road type didn't matter anymore because I had no choice but to move as quickly as possible to finish this thing. That's all I kept thinking as I rode.

I started the climb to Silver City, and I met a couple of guys, one originally from Minnesota, and we chatted a bit. They were very kind and gave me their numbers in case I needed anything once I finished because they lived in town. It was truly incredible how many people I met from Minnesota.

Just like that, I made it to Silver City. It was right around lunchtime, so I stopped to get some lunch and more snacks. Although nearly finished, I still needed food to get through the rest of day. As I sat at McDonald's, I chatted with another rider, someone I hadn't met before, and stayed in town way too long, trying to delay. As I sat there and talked, I knew that once I left McDonald's, I was riding until I was done. Even though I had dreamed of finishing for days, now I wasn't sure I was ready to be done.

When I finally left town, I regretted not leaving sooner, but knowing there was a rider right behind me pushed me to try to finish just a little before him. Leaving Silver City, there was one last climb before the long road to the finish. I saw some chalk drawings on the shoulder of the road near the top of the climb, which were so cute. They read: "Hungry?" "Are you tired of climbing?" The last one was a drawing of a mountain. I thought I should take a picture, but I didn't want to go back after I passed it. The climb wasn't significant or challenging, but when I finished it, I felt so good knowing all the climbing was done. I kept thinking, *I did this; it is all ending, but I did this.*

I turned left and started on the most excellent gravel road over rolling hills. As I looked across the valley, it glowed from the setting sun. It was stunning over the wide-open desert but then I quickly realized that meant I would finish in the dark. Sadly, I wouldn't get the finish I had dreamed of.

Riding on, I noticed the sky behind me had big gray clouds —there was a storm coming my way. I didn't want to get caught in this section with rain because that could slow me down. I knew that once I finished this gravel road, there would be around 60 miles of pavement; I needed to get there before the rain. I just kept thinking over and over again, *You can do this*.

With more determination than I had seen in myself in days, I picked up my speed to stay ahead of the storm cloud. Just as I was finishing the gravel road, there were giant tarantulas everywhere. They were so scary! I had never seen one in person before and don't need to again. I just thought, *I am so glad I didn't have to camp around these things*.

I crossed under the highway and expected to hit pavement but was greeted by a lousy gravel frontage road instead. The road seemed in terrible shape, but it could have been that I was ready to be on the final stretch of pavement—hard to say. After 7 miles, I finally made it to the pavement and knew I wanted to give everything I had to finish. It wasn't like I hadn't been trying up to this point, but I knew with only hours left, I didn't need to save anything for tomorrow. I stopped for a quick minute to lube my chain and empty the rocks out of my shoes, anything to help me go a little faster. Just as I was doing this, the guy from McDonald's went flying by, and I decided I needed to do everything I could to pass him. Not for any reason other than to motivate me to push hard on these last miles, and maybe a little bit because I didn't want him to finish ahead of me.

A border patrol agent at the turn reminded me to watch for animals on the road as the sun set, smiling at me as I rode away. Within minutes, I had caught up to the rider, and after a chat, I kept riding right past him. I was going quickly for the first time in days, at times riding faster than 25 mph until the storm finally caught me.

It was the worst rain I had on my trip. With just hours until the finish, I couldn't believe this was how my ride would end. The rain came in at an angle, and my shoes were full of water within minutes. I still had a tailwind and it was flat, so I kept my speed up, focusing on the road ahead of me. Frustrated and soaked, I felt like nothing was going the way it should. The rain finally stopped just as I reached Hachita, New Mexico. I kept going because I was worried I would get too cold if I stopped. As I continued down the road, a car full of racers were out to cheer, yelling out the windows as they passed. Then a couple of miles later, the guys from the motel in Cuba came by in their van, cheering, and it was starting to feel real. I teared up just thinking about what was about to happen.

Then I saw bison just off the shoulder, and I thought, *It's dark, there are animals, and I still have to make it to the border,* which snapped me back into the moment. I could see the headlight from the other racer, slowly getting farther away, and felt proud that I had made a suitable gap in this final stretch of the ride. As I got closer to the finish, the wind changed, and the road had the slightest grade change of all time. I went from 15 mph to 10 mph. I was beyond frustrated. I had hoped to finish before midnight, and even as hard as I was working, that didn't seem possible anymore. But I kept pushing hard, trying to enjoy every last moment before it was over.

As I kept pedaling down the road, I could see some lights again, but now in front of me and I knew I was close. I started to tear up and then, just like that, I was at the Antelope Wells border crossing. The moment was a blur. There was my family. I was so excited to be done and see the kids and Aaron. There was the Antelope Wells sign I had pictured every time things got hard, and to be in front of it now was overwhelming. I had just ridden the final 170 miles and was exhausted, but somehow full of energy.

There were no tears, which made me laugh because I felt like I had spent the last 25 days crying. Joey sprayed me with champagne, Molly gave me some posters she had made, and we took pictures in front of the sign. I was disappointed it was dark and raining but that was outside of my control, so I focused on the moment. The kids were running around, and Joey talked to frogs in the cattle grate. Molly asked me if I saw the chalk drawings coming out of Silver City and told me that they had drawn them, which made so much sense now. It was nice to laugh with the kids again. I felt overwhelmed, my emotions were up and down. I wanted to be done but I didn't want it to end. Even though not everything went as I had pictured it for months, I needed to just enjoy the moment. I was so proud of what I had done.

I changed into dry clothes as Aaron put my bike on the back of the car. Then I got into the very packed car and realized that it was the first time I had been in a vehicle in almost a month. As we drove back up the road that I had just come down, it felt surreal. I thought about how I didn't have to get up at 5 a.m. the next day and ride all day. Or was it that I didn't *get* to?

As we kept driving, I talked less, and it was quiet, like so many moments during my ride. Reality set in. I was really done with my adventure, the ride of a lifetime, and a race I will never forget. I thought to myself, *I just finished the Great Divide*.

July 6: Informal camping before Lake Roberts, NM, to Antelope Wells, NM

Route Mileage: 2326.51 – 2496.91

Distance: 170.40 miles

Elevation Gain: 7,792 feet

Finish: 25 days, 12 hours and 12 minutes, 2,497 miles

Montana

Idaho

Wyoming

Colorado

5:19
Thursday, July 1
The Great Divide Alarm
Snooze
Stop

THE
GARAGE

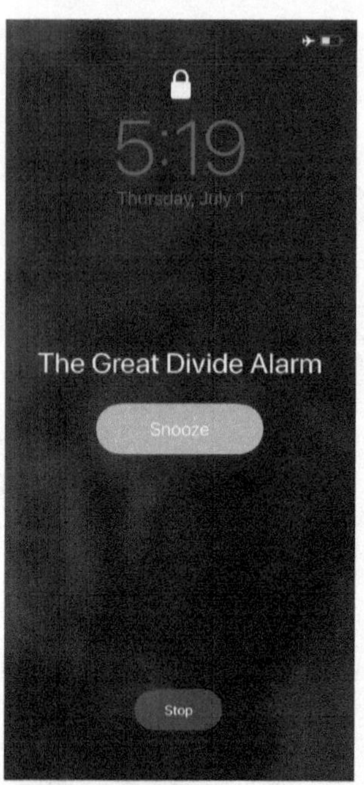

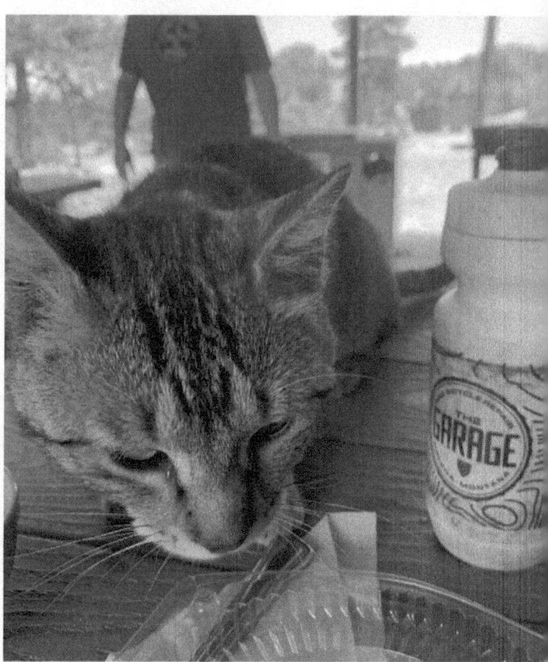

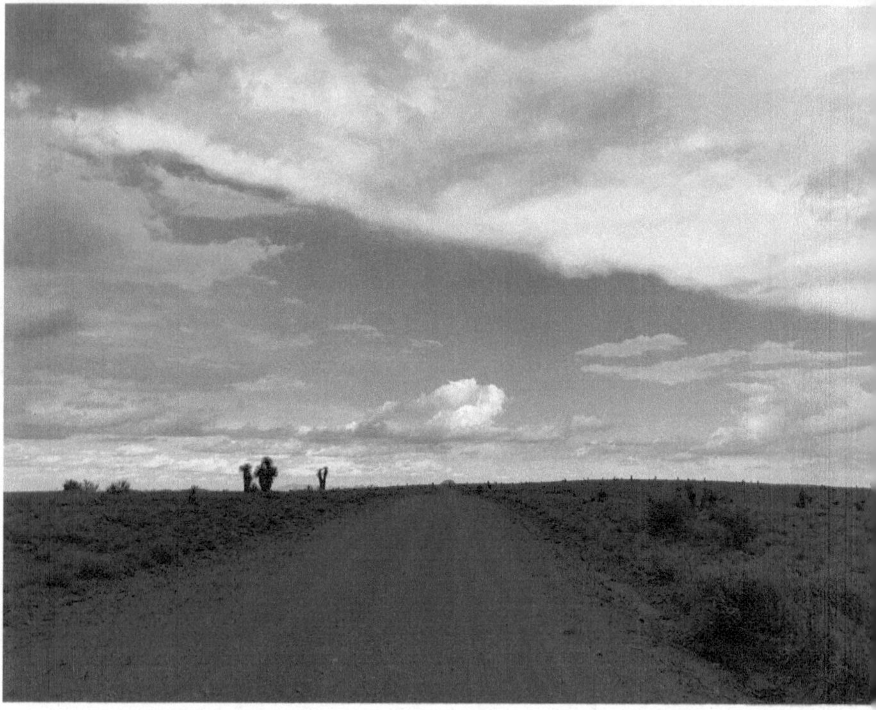

New Mexico

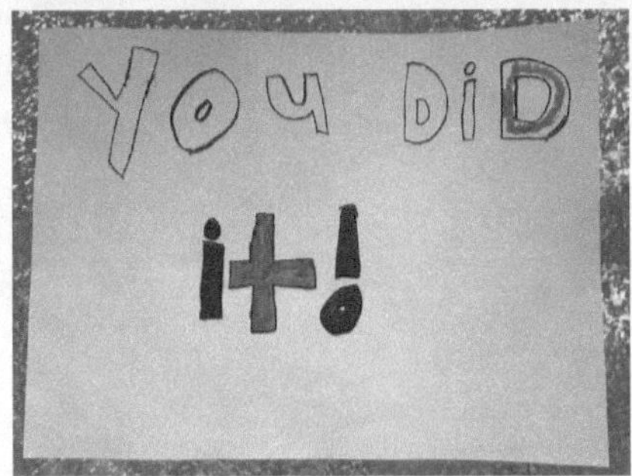

Antelope Wells, New Mexico

The Days After
the Divide

Take Time to Process

After a short night's sleep in a hotel, it felt strange that I didn't have to ride my bike or quickly pack up in the morning. We headed out for a leisurely breakfast, and I felt out of place, waiting for hot food and coffee with my family. It was so nice to be able to relax and eat my food slowly and to be full—but not as full as the day in Pie Town.

My body was confused, feeling like I was still riding and should be eating more to regain my lost weight. When we got back to the hotel, I took the kids to the pool. I put on my swimsuit and looked in the mirror. I didn't recognize my toned legs and a thin torso that I hadn't seen since high school. I sat at the pool, watching the kids splash and play, with many thoughts running through my head about what I had just done.

As I got dressed after the pool, Aaron gave me some shirts that Salsa Cycles had sent to me. He had reached out to them, knowing how disappointed I was about not getting a Divide stem cap for Pie Town. It was so kind of Aaron and Salsa to do something to make me feel special. Then the kids showed me the sweetest video they all put together with congratulations from our friends and family. Trying not to cry, I watched the clips of everyone saying how great I was. I didn't think that I was that special, but they sure did make me feel that way.

We packed up, put the bike back on the car and started north. I felt sad leaving New Mexico and heading back home. It had been such a great trip, and I didn't want it to end. We made a couple of stops on the way home, first to visit a friend in Santa Fe, New Mexico. We chatted about the ride, sharing memories of the route. It was nice to open up and talk about some of the struggles and how crying had helped me during my ride. But talking about the ride just made me want to get back on my bike.

Then, we headed over to our favorite family spot, Salida. It felt so weird to be back where I had just biked to and from only a week or so before. On our way through town, we stopped at Oveja Negra, so I could thank the team in person for the help with my bike bags. One of the owners came by and greeted us with a big smile and a hug. She congratulated me and then asked to see my bags. I was a little embarrassed by my home-sewn bags, but she said they were great and that if I'm ever looking for a job, I could sew for her. It was so kind and it felt so good to have the support of another female bikepacker.

Single Speed Steve drove up and met us for dinner, but first, he took me on a short ride. It felt good to get back on the bike; everything felt normal for a moment. After dinner, we headed to the Family Street Arcade, and the celebration felt official. We played games, cheered, laughed and had a blast. Team Ehlers was back together.

On our drive north, we stopped in Silverthorne before leaving the Divide route for good. We stayed overnight, and in the morning, I asked for a moment alone to sit on the route and process all my feelings. As I sat overlooking the mountains on a trail I had just ridden weeks before, I cried into my hands, overwhelmed with emotions. I took out the camera I had been using to document the ride, and while I might have looked odd to all the people walking by,

I talked to myself and cried. All of the sadness started to set in. I was happy to be back with my family, heading back to what life used to be, but I couldn't help but miss the simplicity of the days on my trip, knowing just what I needed to do every day. It felt unreal; I had spent months and months leading up to this trip, these moments, and just like that, it was over. I felt like I had lost something, but I wasn't sure what. As I rejoined the family, I smiled so much my face hurt. I was relieved to be done, yet I was sad that it was over. *How can this be how I am feeling after finishing? Shouldn't I be overjoyed to be done?*

We continued home, but I tried as hard as I could to get Aaron to delay, asking him to stop just one more night. I wasn't ready to go back to the whole reality of what was waiting for me. I didn't want this high of finishing an adventure to end, but he insisted we had to get home. We finally made it back into Minnesota, and as we drove down Dale Street, my stomach started to hurt. I wanted to stay on the road with my family and be the person I had become over the last four weeks. I didn't want to return to being the grumpy, yelling, short-fused mom and wife I was before, so I thought to myself, *You have to make the choice to change.*

We pulled into the driveway, and there were all my friends and family waiting to congratulate me. What a surprise! I was overjoyed with the support and the number of people who came to the party. I had hardly seen anyone in over a year because of the pandemic, and now everyone was here. I looked weird, not recognizing myself in the mirror, wondering what people would think. I was happy but also had a feeling I couldn't explain and I didn't want anyone to know about. I felt proud of what I had accomplished but also sad, which made me feel guilty. I should be enjoying this moment but it was difficult because I felt like I had so much to share and wasn't sure how. As I showed people my bike and talked about my trip, I started to feel better, but I missed being alone and knowing precisely what I needed to do every day.

When I said goodbye to our friends and family, I took a picture with each person so I could remember who came because I was in such a daze. Sitting on the deck with Aaron, Katie and Brian, I finally felt like I could relax. I looked out into the yard, snuggled with our puppy, listening to everyone talk but not hearing anything, not sure what tomorrow would bring, but knowing things would be different. I was different. I thought about my time away and reflected on what the days had taught me. I realized I hadn't lost anything; I had gained a fresh perspective on life. Care for myself, my body and my mind, and everything else will fall into place.

One Year After
the Divide

Enjoy the Race, the Ride, the Adventure

Waking up, day after day, I continued to be amazed that I had somehow managed to cover 2,500 miles of unfamiliar terrain in unpredictable weather in just over 25 days. Despite feeling exhausted due to lack of sleep and insufficient food, I pushed myself to complete the Great Divide Race, when over half of the people who start the race don't finish it.

I was the third woman to get to Antelope Wells in the 2021 race, but when I told people that I had averaged just under 100 miles of riding a day, the reactions I got varied from, "That's not just anything, 100 miles is so much" to "100 miles a day is good." In the very competitive racing world, 100 miles a day is just okay, which kept this question in my mind: Did I *race* the Divide?

I had called it *the ride* for months leading up to leaving and even during the first weeks of riding, because I had thought racing meant you were fast and trying to finish first. While that is one definition, racing can also mean to complete a task in the shortest amount of time. I will never be fast, but I wasn't racing to win, I was racing myself. Pushing myself to complete the ride as quickly as I could, not giving up when it was hard, and giving myself the opportunity to succeed no matter what anyone said. Racing meant putting forth my best effort every day, challenging myself to see what I could do and what I could learn from the experience, and how I could overcome obstacle after obstacle without losing focus on my goal. I rode long days with little sleep and was exhausted every day. I climbed in a granny gear and did not descend quickly. But *the race* kept me pushing every day, through exhaustion and tears, to meet my goal of finishing the Divide.

I remember I asked Aaron a couple of nights before we left, "What if I can only do 40-60 miles a day?" And he responded, "Then you do 40-60 a day, and you bike for 25 days, just like we planned." The idea of finishing the entire route was a fantastic goal, but there was no coming home early; I wanted to ride my bike and be alone to learn about myself.

Every single day, I asked myself: *Why am I even doing this? Is this still fun?* There were so many times I would push my bike, take a nap, find something to eat, check for cell service, all because I didn't feel like biking anymore. I called hotels and restaurants to check on their hours and make reservations when before the race, I couldn't even get myself to call and order a pizza. I talked to strangers and made friends. Through all those moments, I persevered because I wanted to be out there. I wanted to do this for myself: to push myself, put myself outside my comfort zone and see what I could do.

From the start, I called this ride an adventure. It, indeed, was an adventure that turned into a race. But I will always remember it as an adventure, not just me riding my bike but the commitment, the build-up to getting to the start and then accomplishing my goal.

During this adventure, I learned that I like to take things at my own pace. I enjoy taking time away from the noise of life to learn something new and recenter myself. The most important lesson I learned was that the time away from my family helped us grow in ways I never knew were possible. While I love my kids, I always say

I'm not a kid person. This time away gave us the space we needed to miss each other. I realized we don't need to be arguing about the little things, like not doing the dishes the moment I ask. It's just not as important as I might think. I need to enjoy the time I have with them and every moment they still want to hang out with me. This adventure gave me the ability to see that I can step away from work, the kids, Aaron and be on my own. It reminded me that I am more than a mom, a wife, an employee—I am my own person.

I am so proud of what I did. I rode my bicycle across five U.S. states from Canada to Mexico, through dozens of mountain passes; from pavement to gravel roads to snowy trails; in rain, wind and 100-degree days in Montana and 35-degree nights in Colorado; with breathtaking landscapes, starry nights, sunsets and sunrises. I met the most wonderful people and had the most terrific support from my family and fantastic husband every day back home. I am lucky to have been able to do this race: Getting out there, doing something for myself, learning new life lessons along the way and growing as a person was the ultimate win.

Epilogue

Never Stop Exploring

Bikepacking the Divide seems so similar to birthing a baby. I spent nine months preparing, reading and learning all about it. I spent hours in the hospital, in pain, tired and ready for it to be over, and then Joey was born. No more pain, just a snuggly baby, and I was so happy. A few months later, I forgot all about the nine long months of carrying a baby and the pain of birth and got pregnant again.

Somehow, bikepacking was the same. After finishing the Divide, I wanted to do it again, but I didn't know why. I had spent months planning and then was exhausted and tired every single day. But it was exactly what I needed. I came home from the Divide refreshed, happier and ready to be my best self for those around me, and my story didn't entirely end there.

I decided I would try something not so long but more difficult and race the Colorado Trail. Before the Colorado Trail Race (CTR), I spent a month in an Airbnb in Salida, Colorado, teaching myself how to mountain bike. I asked locals for the best trails to ride. It was such a good feeling to be able to do that and, this time, I wasn't even scared. I spent my evenings riding up and down the backyard trails of Salida, practicing single-track riding and learning how to push myself to bike up climbs and not just walk. I took time for myself, relaxing and reading books by the river before taking on another adventure.

I headed to Denver, Colorado, where I started the CTR, and spent the next 14 days wondering what I was doing out there. I was in way over my head, without enough mountain bike experience, just trying to do my best. I kept moving forward, riding my bike when I could, pushing my bike up mountain pass after mountain pass more than I would like to admit. The single track was scarier than I anticipated, and I couldn't figure out how to conquer my fear of the edge. I crashed, I cried and, of course, I napped. Somehow I finished the CTR. It was a reality check that I can do things I put my mind to, but maybe I shouldn't.

Now, I had done two major bikepacking races in the United States, and someone asked me on my drive home if I would ride the Arizona Trail and finish the Triple Crown of bikepacking. While part of me knew I had to do it, part of me screamed NO! I didn't feel ready to be back on my bike. I wasn't ready for the sleep deprivation, which had become my biggest challenge.

But, when I realized I was turning 34, the same age my dad was when he died, I knew I needed to do it right away. Over the years of my adulthood, there were so many milestones I feared. When Joey turned 3, the same age my little sister was when my dad passed, I felt sad. Looking at my own child, I realized how my sister couldn't really have understood what was happening. Then, when Molly reached the age I was when my dad passed, I cried for days, thinking about what it felt like to lose my dad. Her bond with Aaron is so lovely, and I never want to think about what it would look like if he were gone. Then there were so many days where I wondered if I would make it past 34. I never thought I was dying, but the idea of having more days alive than he did scared me. I wanted to take advantage of those days. I wanted to finish the Triple Crown before I was 35. That was my new dream.

I decided to ride the Arizona Trail as an Individual Time Trial (ITT). Excited for this next adventure, I headed to Arizona and spent a week with Erik, who I met during the Divide, and his family, getting ready for the Spring 2023 ITT. Erik took me to the start at the Mexican border where we camped overnight before I started the following morning. I took off with plenty of time to ride the Arizona Trail, because I had planned my start in mid-May around a trail closure in the Grand Canyon. While I was sad to not be part of the race, it was a great experience to be racing by myself and knowing there were no other riders out there and I was truly alone. And, it was nice to not have to worry about the miles I had to cover every day, the way I had to on the other two races. The time of year was a little more challenging with less water available and hotter days as I got closer to June, but it was what worked for me. As I started the race, I took my time, acclimating to the heat and enjoying the landscapes of Arizona.

While biking one hot afternoon, I received a message that the opening of the North Kaibab trail in the Grand Canyon was delayed. I was frustrated, upset and incredibly heartbroken when I heard this news. I had come to finish this series and this was not part of my plan. I read the message multiple times, processing what it said. I couldn't believe this was happening when I was trying to finish my bikepacking Triple Crown. I had no choice but to continue. Frustrated that I couldn't find the trail amongst the huge rocks, I pushed my bike and cried.

Hours later, I arrived in Summerhaven, Arizona, and sat and cried some more outside a community center. Trying to pull myself together, I thought: *There is nothing I can do, this is out of my control, and all I can do now is finish what I started, as much of the Arizona Trail as is open.* Just like with the Divide, I needed to accept that my ride wouldn't be the full route, but that shouldn't stop me. I thought, *If I am only doing this because I want others to acknowledge what I am doing, then why am I out here to begin with?* I pulled myself together because finishing this race was about finishing for me, even if I'm not an official Triple Crown finisher.

I started back down the trail, remembering that for every hard moment, there is a good one. *This is just another obstacle you have to overcome*, I thought. Days later, I arrived at the Grand Canyon and portaged my bike to the bottom of the canyon, the official finish of my race. Carrying my bike on my back, because you can't ride on the trails in National Parks, felt like an unusual and special way to finish my cycling race. After arriving at Phantom Ranch, I took a selfie as "Proof of Finish." As I stood there, alone with my bike on my back, I felt proud. There was no one there to cheer me in or recognize what I'd just done. I didn't have cell reception to call Aaron and the kids to celebrate my journey, but I felt happy that I had accomplished what I had set out to do.

I was planning to turn around and spend the next 10 hours hiking out of the canyon so I could be with my family when a Park Ranger walked by and suggested I stay since it was hot, and they had already had to do a helicopter rescue. I found some people to camp with and relaxed, enjoying the river flowing through the canyon and all the thoughts flowing through my head.

I couldn't believe what I'd done. I had finished some of the hardest bikepacking routes in the United States in just two years. I had gone from a casual bike commuter to a bikepacking Triple Crown finisher. My life had changed so much, in ways I didn't know it needed to change. I realized I need to be thankful for every day I have to spend with family, go on adventures and live my life. I thank my body for allowing me to do these things, my family for supporting me and my job for providing the funds to do it. Completing these adventures meant so much to me. I was reminded that my Papa's life was too short, and if I learned anything after the Divide, it was how important it is to live in the moment because we don't know what our lives will look like tomorrow.

As I hiked out of the canyon the next day with my bike on my back, I felt like a celebrity with people asking me questions or wanting to take my picture and the Park Rangers checking in to make sure I was okay. I thought about how special the Grand Canyon was for me. On that family vacation with my Papa when I was kid, we stopped at the Grand Canyon during an April snowstorm—there's a picture of all of us kids and our cousins in front of the Canyon and nothing but a white sky. It always made me laugh that we went to the Grand Canyon in Arizona and got snow.

Then, Aaron took me back to the Grand Canyon on our honeymoon, and we arrived on a cold January day with a snowstorm. I couldn't believe it; I could see nothing but a white sky again. When we woke up the next day, I saw for the first time the stunning canyon. I was in awe of the magnificent sight of the deep canyon high over the Colorado River with all the layers of rocks. A couple of years later, when I was pregnant with Joey, we went back to hike and camp at Phantom Ranch, right at the bottom next to the river, where I had just stayed the night before.

Hours later, I finally made it close to the rim. I could no longer see the river; the desert slowly changed from cool to hot. As I approached the top and walked around the final switchback, I could see Joey, Molly and Aaron. I couldn't wait to get the bike off my back and hug them all. I knew I was done but when I finally took those last steps, I could no longer feel the weight of the bike on my back or the pain in my legs. It brought tears to my eyes. I had done it. I was done. This was *my* finish.

The Great Divide, 2021

Photo by Aaron Ehler

Colorado Trail Race, 2022

Photo by Eszter Horanyi

Arizona Trail, 2023

Photo by Derrick Lytle

Bikepacking Notes

Bikepacking the Great Divide

What food did you carry? How much stuff was actually on your bike with you?

I carried a stove with oatmeal and ramen noodles as backup food so I could at least eat if something strange happened. Otherwise, I carried snacks, including gummy candy, gas station pastries, nuts and bars. I didn't vary too much from those foods because they worked for me. I also would try to find restaurants with burritos or sandwiches because then I could eat one and take one for later. I was always looking for breakfast at a place to sit down. For the first few days, I carried everything on my bike, and then I hit the Basin and used my lightweight backpack to carry extra food. Sometimes I would put my clothes in the bag because they were light and put the food on the bike. I used that for days to carry extra food because I didn't feel like I had enough. It became like a heat box for me during the day. The backpack was a great option to carry more food on long stretches and take it off when it wasn't needed. I didn't count calories or track what I was eating very well but maybe I should have.

Some of my favorite things to carry:

- Pastries—anything and everything I could find, especially apple pies
- Nuts, trail mix and lots of cashews and Pearson's Salted Nut Rolls

- Rice crispy bars and cereal bars

- Chips and salty snacks

- Beef jerky with pepper jack cheese

- Peach rings

- My emergency food that was on the bike at all times: coffee, oatmeal and ramen noodles

What was the bike setup?

- Bike: Titanium Salsa Fargo, SRAM Force Axs, Areobars with Bar-end Blips, 10-52 cassette, 36t Camo Wolftooth Chainring, Shimano Pedals, Mezcal 2.5 Tires with Tyrewiz Tire Pressure Monitors, WTB KOM Tough Rims, DT Swiss 350 Rear Hub and SON Dynamo Front Hub, with a kLite Headlight and Tail Light, with two additional tail lights and a WahooRoam for GPS

- Extra Parts and Tools: Axs Batteries (3) and Charger, multi-tool, Wolftooth Chain Tool, tire levers, small floor pump, bottle of lube, spare tubs (2), bolts, shoe cleats, brake pads (2), tire boot, patch kit, tape, zip ties, velcro, derailleur hanger, Ziploc bag, sewing kit, master links, spokes, chain, Pocket Juice

What gear did you carry on your bike and what did you wear?

I tried to keep only the necessities because space was limited, and I had the following with me the entire trip.

- Clothing: helmet, buff, prescription sunglasses, shirt, arm warmers, fleece sweater, rain jacket, packable jacket, down hoodie, warm gloves (45NRTH), rain mitts, bike gloves, bike shorts, leggings, rain shorts, underwear, clip-in bike shoes, heavyweight wool socks, lightweight wool socks (2).

- Sleeping System: Outdoor Research Helium bivy, DIY sleeping bag with Sea to Summit liner, Nemo sleeping pad, Sea to Summit pillow

- Electronics: iPhone, SPOT GPS tracker, AfterShokz headphones, Airpods, Anker Power Banks-10K and 5L, USB-C to Lightning, MicroUSB cables (2), 2032 lithium batteries, AA lithium batteries, AnkerPD USB-C, Anker Double Wall charger

- Toiletries: Body Glide for Her, Baby Bum Chapstick, baby wipes, sunblock, small first aid kit, hair comb, tampons, toothbrush, toothpaste, contacts, contact solution

- Other: driver's license, emergency contact card, cash, bear spray

- Cooking: pot, stove, silverware, collapsible cup

Would you change anything on the bike? What wouldn't you change?

- The most significant change I would make is that I would have a way to mount my phone on the bike. It would have been nice for navigating some of the larger towns. Also, if my WahooRoam had broken and I had needed to use my phone for navigation, it would have been nice to have a place to mount it.

- I did add an extra water bottle, so having four bottles instead of three from the start would be another change I would make. I would likely put the sleep roll on the handlebar and the "junk bag" in the back.

- What I loved the most on the bike were my Tyrewiz Pressure monitors because they displayed my tire pressure on the Wahoo, which was amazing. I didn't need to worry about what my pressure was every day and I couldn't blame moving slowly on anything but myself.

- I also loved the WahooRoam. Moving from the Element to the Roam was a great decision; the bigger screen and more room to display data fields was beneficial. I also loved the climbing screen and being able to look at the elevation of what I had done and what I had left to do every single day. It helped me to know what was coming, knowing I would do it either way, but being able to mentally prepare for those challenging climbs and then knowing when or what part of my day it would happen.

- Lastly, I carried a little fanny pack. I changed what I carried in there a little along the ride, but for the most part, I always had my ID and wallet on my body. I carried my cue sheets in there and the notes from the kids and Aaron. It was an excellent place to add anything I was worried about getting wet. Some people wear jerseys with pockets, and this was similar, but I could take it off. It didn't bother me and was a great way to keep important things close to my body.

Would you do anything differently?

- I would figure out a better strategy for rain and my feet. I carried my 45NRTH winter gloves, which were terrific, but my feet got very wet when it rained. It wasn't like they were cold, but it wasn't enjoyable, so I would think of something to help with that situation. I found out very quickly that I don't like wet feet.

- Maybe I would try not to use a blow-up sleeping pad and find a foam rollup one. I was tired and lazy and stopped inflating the pad by the end of the trip. I could have used the warmth and padding but I was just too tired to do it.

- I would have been a lot more careful with food in bear country. I thought I was doing a good job, but I could have done much better, and I'm lucky nothing happened.

- Finding a new headlamp that I was sure would last a little longer is something else I would do. I found it too hard to ride at night with only one light, and my dynamo light didn't stay bright enough if I was going slowly.

- I would carry two pairs of padded shorts. When it's hot, they get dirty quickly, which caused me so much discomfort that I had to stop a lot. I would take on the weight and space to have a second pair for those times.

- Also, I would find better ways to stay awake at night. I had a hard time booking a hotel in the morning because I was not sure if I would or could make it there. Maybe I would do better about committing to a room and pushing myself to get there.

Lastly, would you, do this again?

I hope so. The hardest part was the mental side, the easy part was the riding, and the riding wasn't easy. Because of that, it's hard to think how I could push through the mental barriers for a second time. I think the second time I do anything, I get in my head and think: *There is no reason I can't do it. I've already done it once before, so why is it so difficult?*

But it's not that simple. There are many factors that can change from year to year: my body, my training, my gear. And so much of this race has to do with the weather. I feel lucky I had the weather I did for the race, but I think: *What if ... What if it rained more? What if I had snow? What if I had peanut butter mud? How would I be able to push through that? Would I be able to do it mentally?* So, would I do it again? I think so, but I would have to approach it with the understanding that I'm not doing the same race again.

Interested in a little more about my adventures?

• Check out this podcast done by the amazing folks on the Chasing Tomorrow Podcast on the Great Divide

> Ep. #61 - MTB racing from Canada to Mexico with Mary Ehlers

• Head over to The Town Bicycle and read a great article by Eszter Horanyi on the Colorado Trail

> https://thetownbicycle.com/last-woman-standing-mary-ehlers-and-the-2022-ctr/

• Listen to my unfiltered thoughts during the AZT on mtbcast.com

> http://mtbcast.com/site2/?s=Mary+Ehlers&x=0&y=0

Acknowledgments

When I began writing, I never imagined it would be as rewarding as riding the Divide itself. This was supposed to be a journal of my story of riding the Divide that I could leave to Joey and Molly for when I'm old and can't remember it anymore. But writing my thoughts brought light to all the lessons I learned along the way. Although it took more time than I thought it would, I enjoyed every minute of the process, but it was the collaboration with all the people who helped make this book readable that brought me the most joy.

I couldn't have done this without my dear friend Julie. She has read this book more times than me and continues to be more than happy to read another draft, fixing the same mistakes I keep making and always asking when I would send a new version. Our lunch dates, coffee outings and her constant support mean more to me than I can express.

Aaron, Joey and Molly, I wouldn't have done this without your support.

Aaron, thank you for giving me the space and time to sit down and be back in my own bubble. Your willingness to let me ask questions about my ride or to remind me of places I rode or things that happened to me meant so much and made sure I included all the memories I want to keep forever.

Joey, from making yourself dinner to checking in with me about how the book was going, your encouragement meant so much. Thank you for giving me space to work, even if that was just so you could go play video games. :)

And Molly, I'm amazed by your ability to encourage me during this writing process. Whether it was taking the rough draft to school to read or listening to me reading it out loud on the couch, you were always willing to help. Thank you for sitting with me on my office floor just so we could "hang out," and for your best friend, Maggie, who kept you busy and distracted at sleepovers so I could work late without feeling guilty.

Thank you, Sydney, for pushing through the early stage of my writing. Your comments made me smile so big, and it was so fun to have someone I didn't know say they loved it. When you asked if you could have a copy for your classroom, you inspired me to make this the best I could.

Theo, thanks for the positive and constructive feedback. Thanks for picking up the phone and calling to see how things were going and to discuss the project.

To my sisters: Katie, who called and told me she was reading the book to my nephews, thank you for the honest feedback about how reading it out loud was "hard at times." And my little sister, Melanie, who took time away from her own project, thank you for showing your support.

And to all my friends at Fjällräven, thank you for listening to me talk endlessly about the book and for giving me ideas on how I could make it better.

A special thanks to my BuyNothing neighbor who will never know the impact they had with their gift of a couch. It was the perfect place for Dakota and me to sit and work, so I could always have my puppy nearby, and just what I needed so I could make my office into a place I would love to work.

With the help of all of you, my journal became a story. Your support helped me bring my story to life. While I never imagined sharing my story in this way, I'm so grateful for each and every one of you.

As Molly says, "Bikes are awesome and so are the people who ride them." I hope you all find your own adventure.

Mary Ehlers

A wife, mother, daughter, sister, aunt, woman, friend, adventurer and now .... a cyclist.

www.ingramcontent.com/pod-product-compliance
Lightning Source LLC
Chambersburg PA
CBHW051431130726
47987CB00005B/1998